LifeParticle Meditation

LifeParticle
meditation

a practical guide
to healing &
transformation

ILCHI LEE

**BEST
LIFE**

BEST Life Media
6560 State Route 179, Suite 114
Sedona, AZ 86351
www.bestlifemedia.com
877.504.1106

This publication contains the opinions and ideas of the author. Through this book, the author and publisher are not engaged in rendering medical, health, or any other kind of personal service. The reader should consult his or her medical, health, or other professional before adopting any of the suggestions in the book. The author and publisher disclaim any liability arising directly or indirectly from the use and application of any of the book's contents.

First paperback edition: June 2013
Library of Congress Control Number: 2013936312
ISBN-13: 978-1-935127-59-8
Photos page 29, 123 © Office Masaru Emoto, LLC
Cover and interior design by Malou Leontsinis. Illustrations by Al Choi.

• • •

There is a life that exists of itself,
by itself, and in itself.
We are the flowers that blossomed from this life,
the phenomena created by this life.

• • •

CONTENTS

• • •

The innumerable phenomena of life
are temporary manifestations of LifeParticles.
Once we know that everything comes and goes
in a flux of LifeParticles,
we can watch ourselves and the world with tranquility.

• • •

Author's Introduction

Though our world is saturated with ceaseless external stimulation, it's amazing but true that boredom is still one of the things most feared by modern people today. One popular "fix" is getting caught up in all sorts of entertainment to distract ourselves. Unconsciously, we turn on our TVs, spend hours in thoughtless Internet shopping, indulge in alcohol or foods that damage our health, and search for someone with whom we can spend time. However, boredom soon sets in because, in most cases, such activities provide only temporary satisfaction, and we're off in search of yet another stimulus to satisfy our weary souls.

In fact, it seems that we seek stimulation all the time. Why? Without stimulation, we feel insecure, because that's how we assure ourselves that we are still alive. Without stimulation, we cannot feel our existence. The main reason we continually seek this external stimulation is a sense of restlessness or insecurity.

However, the real cause of restlessness is not the lack of stimulation outside. It is the hollow emptiness inside. Because it is deep inside, it cannot be filled with any external stimulation for more than a short while. This hollow can be filled only when we find the "real stuff" inside of us.

Possessions, outer appearances, social status, personal relationships, fluctuating emotions, and countless random thoughts do not matter. Only when you encounter that something that rests serenely in the deepest part of your being, and transcends all these things, are you able to feel genuine satisfaction and inner peace. Although different individuals might describe it in different ways, I think that, at its core, it is the feeling of *life* itself.

There is within me the feeling of my heart beating right now, of precious life energy flowing within me . . . can you try to feel this life energy flowing within you, too? When we discover this within ourselves, our lives recover vitality like dry land after a welcome rain, and we begin to blossom beautifully and to bear rich fruit.

The purpose of this book is to help you discover that subtle yet powerful feeling of life through LifeParticle Meditation. By helping you to feel and apply LifeParticles, it will empower you to have a life full of vitality and significance and to create the life you truly want.

LifeParticles is a concept that expresses the world I experienced about thirty years ago at the peak of a spiritual journey I took to discover who I really was. What I saw then, while in a deep state of meditation, were rapidly vibrating and moving grains of bright light filling a space that spread out infinitely in all directions. The self I perceived at that time was particles of bright light itself. It wasn't just me; everything around me looked that way. There was no boundary or separation at all between me, things around, and the space beyond. I was the energy of the cosmos and the mind of the cosmos. Those brilliant grains of life that are energy and consciousness, and life itself, are what I call "LifeParticles."

What was fascinating was that this world I saw through meditation is very similar to the world we see in modern physics when we continue to split matter until we reach the level of elementary particles. The smallest units of matter and energy making up the cosmos that physics has discovered so far are elementary particles. These elementary particles are not fixed, but are constantly changing according to the consciousness of the observer. The reality that modern science discovered is telling us that matter and consciousness are one inseparable whole.

LifeParticle Meditation is based on two very important realizations. The first is that you are LifeParticles; the second is that LifeParticles are at your command. LifeParticles are the essence of who you are and compose your body and consciousness right now, at this very moment; at the same time, they are yours to directly feel and apply in your daily life.

Be sure to remember this: You are LifeParticles, and LifeParticles are at your command.

If you experience LifeParticles, and at that level enter your consciousness to watch yourself and the world, everything will look brand-new. You are LifeParticles, and the people you love and hate are all LifeParticles, too. The sky, the ground, the flowers, the trees, all things in the universe are waving and vibrating as LifeParticles.

Within the world of LifeParticles, the dichotomous

boundaries separating self and other, subject and object, being and non-being, have ceased to exist, and you will perceive one whole world in which separation and discrimination also do not exist. You will escape from the matrix of the material world, in which you appear to be separate, solidly fixed, and limited, and you will discover a great secret that will allow you to create the reality you truly desire.

Those who discover and master this secret are the alchemists of life. The good news is that becoming such an alchemist is definitely not difficult; in fact, anyone can master the art.

I would like to help you open your eyes to the LifeParticle world of infinite potential and creation through this book. I earnestly hope that you will experience directly the principles by which LifeParticles operate and the phenomena they create, and that you will be able to actively apply them in your life.

Try to begin your day with the bright light of LifeParticles, increase your focus on your work and the quality of your personal relationships with LifeParticles, and charge your body and mind with LifeParticles when you go to sleep. Brightly shining LifeParticles will activate your body's natural healing ability and bring you a bright smile and overflowing vitality. Once your brain is awakened by the positive energy of LifeParticles, significant change will inevitably come to your consciousness, energy, and life.

The reason I am able to say this with such confidence is that I have seen countless people experience amazing healing and transformation through LifeParticle Meditation. LifeParticle Meditation is based on universal principles and laws of energy. Consequently, following those principles will allow anyone, anytime and anywhere, to experience their effects—without exception!

This book, as a practical guide, is focused on the everyday application of LifeParticle Meditation. If you would like to learn more about LifeParticle Theory, and about the diverse stories of people who have experienced LifeParticle Meditation, please see the movie *Change: The LifeParticle Effect*, and its companion volume, another one of my books.

I believe that LifeParticle Meditation will bring you health, happiness, and inner peace. LifeParticles are the essence and the very best of who you are. At the moment you become one with LifeParticles through meditation, the very best of you spreads out like waves into your life and into the world. This is why I have great certainty that LifeParticle Meditation will bring more hope, beauty, and goodness to the world, as well as to your personal life.

You have great power to change your life and the world. We can change the world, which is made up of LifeParticles, and ourselves, for we are also those very LifeParticles. We truly can do that. Truly.

I send you LifeParticles with love and gratitude.

May everyone be happy.

Ilchi Lee
Sedona, Arizona, March 2013

Includes a LifeParticle meditation card

LifeParticle
meditation

a practical guide
to healing &
transformation

ILCHI LEE *New York Times* bestselling author

Experience fundamental awakening about life and yourself

LifeParticles are what **Ilchi Lee** calls the elementary particles that are the essence of everything. They are matter, energy, and consciousness combined. When you access the world of LifeParticles, you tap into a vast reservoir of vitality, love, and limitless creative potential. LifeParticle Meditation is an amazingly simple way to master the art of accessing this world and discovering who you really are.

With detailed instructions, learn to directly feel and apply **LifeParticles** in your daily life for whatever you wish.

- Be more peaceful & centered
- Discover the power of your mind
- Create the situations & things you want
- Help others wherever they are

Author **Ilchi Lee** draws upon a lifetime of meditation experience, information from the realms of science & spirituality, and stories from practitioners of LifeParticle Meditation around the world to bring you this profound yet practical meditation method.

BEST
LIFE

A companion book to the film *Change: The LifeParticle Effect*
www.bestlifemedia.com

chapter 1

What Are LifeParticles?

One of the best ways to appreciate the astonishing power of LifeParticles is through understanding the effects of its practice on the lives of real people.

In June 2011, during a LifeParticle workshop I was giving at a retreat center near Nagoya, Japan, I participated in a collaborative healing session in which LifeParticles were sent to a fifty-five-year-old woman, Yahata Chieko, and a few others. We hoped in our hearts that, with over one hundred people participating, those members who had suffered poor health would truly be helped. And, in our deepest hearts, we were even hoping for a miracle.

Yahata's life had been difficult; she had lived with disease since she was very young. At the age of seven, diphtheria had inflamed her throat and hindered breathing; traumatic memories of that time had caused a fear of suffocating, which had kept her from breathing deeply her whole life.

At the age of seventeen, the anesthesia received during an appendectomy somehow didn't work. After the surgery, her stomach continued to hurt, which caused her body to tense up and distort, and pain was created in other areas. Since her body's autonomic regulation wasn't working properly, she suffered from depression. Her continual poor health, which doctors could not attribute to any disease, was finally diagnosed as early-onset Parkinson's syndrome. On the bright side, Yahata says that she was actually happy to finally know the name of her affliction.

Yahata's health deteriorated to the point where she had trouble even walking, but that didn't keep her from going to the library. She was eagerly seeking something, although she didn't know what it would be until she found it. One day, though, she did find what she was looking for, and it just happened to be LifeParticle Meditation and training.

When she first began the training, people described her in the following way: "Her body would tremble a lot, and she was very wobbly when she walked, always bent over and using a cane. She fell down often and so much that we felt we should go and help her along. She couldn't even stand with her feet together and, when she walked, she would use only the front part of her feet, so that the soles of her feet never completely touched the ground. She seemed to be walking while floating in the air."

The day of this collaborative LifeParticle healing, over a hundred participants, as I said earlier, were standing in a circle, and those in poor health entered the inner circle. Yahata was one of them. The participants and I sent LifeParticles to those who were ill, earnestly desiring that they be healed. As the atmosphere gradually intensified, I felt the hot healing energy of LifeParticles going into action.

That's when it happened. Yahata, who had been sitting in a chair, suddenly got up, stood there with her feet together, and started walking without even using her cane! The soles of her feet touched the ground, she walked without falling over, and then, to everyone's surprise, she started to dance, raising one leg and then the other. The participants cheered and applauded as they watched her dancing so happily, weaving in and out of the participants as they stood in the circle. Many were deeply moved and shed tears of joy when they saw how happy she was.

It was a day of wonder that Yahata says she will never forget. Here is how she described it: "I was able, after forty years, to stand with my feet together, and also with the soles of my feet touching the floor. And then I tried walking. And the soles of my feet touched the floor, which was completely different from the way I had been walking before then. For me, it is truly a *miracle*!"

Becoming emotional, she paused for a few moments, unable to speak, and then continued, "When the soles of my feet touched the ground, a really wonderful feeling of happiness rose up from the bottoms of my feet. I thought, I can be this happy just by walking with the soles of my feet touching the floor! It was truly a happiness that I felt for the first time since I was born. I was really envious of people who could walk properly with their feet flat on the ground. Now I can walk and feel the happiness. Although some say they are unhappy because they don't have this or that, I think human beings are already plenty happy just by standing with the soles of their feet touching the earth and being able to breathe; and there is no greater happiness than that!"

"LifeParticles are love," Yahata said emphatically. "What I felt was the love of those people; that was it. My heart was so joyful and peaceful, and I knew, this is what love is!"

Yahata's story is not the only story of miraculous healing. Many amazing experiences, some big and some small, are happening for those people all over the world who practice LifeParticle Meditation. I have been fascinated by the depth and diversity of the incredible stories told by people who have made LifeParticle Meditation an important part of their lives. In fact, the word *miracle* pops up all the time in people's descriptions of their experiences with LifeParticles!

Do you believe in miracles? Phenomena that are difficult to understand or explain rationally and seem supernatural are commonly called "miracles." But what if such miraculous occurrences happen not to one or two people, but frequently to many people? Wouldn't it mean that, behind such phenomena, universal laws are at work?

I've spent a lot of time exploring the universal laws behind such miracles of healing. In the course of my exploration of my own inner workings, the wisdom of the ancients, the experience of many people, and scientific findings, I've come to understand the unseen energy principles that transform the "impossible" into reality. And I've developed meditation techniques that harness these principles so that, rather than just hoping for a random "miracle," you can actually manifest them consciously and proactively in your life.

Awakening to Universal Principles

The crux of these energy principles is LifeParticles. To help further explain what LifeParticles are, I'd like to describe my first major awakening through my own meditation.

Growing up, I was plagued by the questions "Who am I? Why am I here? Why am I alive?" Perhaps such existential questions were instinctive, especially to someone born in 1950 at the beginning of the Korean War. However, they came to the forefront after my friend drowned while we were swimming in a reservoir near my home in a small village near Cheonan, South Korea. Afterward, I suffered intense fear and anxiety thinking that I could also die suddenly, at any time, without knowing the real reason for my existence in the world.

I didn't find an answer to my questions until I was fully grown and married with two sons. Although I had attained a career and a family, I still felt there was something more to life. Determined to find the answers to the questions that filled my mind, I decided to go to a meditation place on Mount Moak in South Korea; my plan was not to eat, sleep, or lie down until I had those answers. I had already read books, developed my mental and physical strength through years of martial arts, and knew how to manage my body's energy through breathing and qigong. I felt prepared; and I also felt as if there was no other way but this for me.

After five days on the mountain, I was no longer able to control my body, and drowsiness overwhelmed me. Seven episodes of extreme circumstances I thought I could no longer endure finally did pass and I found myself half asleep, somewhere between the worlds of the conscious and unconscious, and gazing into both.

At one point, I experienced such intense pain in my head that it felt like it would split open. I attempted all sorts of things to relieve the pain, even standing on my head and sitting on the edge of a cliff. Nothing worked, so I gave up fighting the pain. My heart then felt lighter, and I was able to sit still in a lotus posture and observe my pain while I controlled my breathing. With that surrender, a thought came to me like a flash of light. "Who is it that's in pain? What hurts is my head. It's just my body in pain, not me." Then I heard what sounded like an explosion, but the explosion was also in my head. Soon, I realized that it was actually an explosion of all the ideas that had limited my being to my body and the material world.

The pain was replaced by peace, gratitude, and love. I felt as though I was at the center of endless cosmic space. Everything around me, including my body, became a field of brilliantly shining and vibrating bits of light—what I now call LifeParticles. Solid form and boundaries between one thing and another ceased to exist.

Then an inner voice asked the question I had pondered for so long: "Who am I?"

A reply burst from inside me:

"I am Cosmic Energy."

"I am Cosmic Mind."

At that moment, I realized that I am the same consciousness as all that exists and the same consciousness watching all that exists. And I am made of the same energy as all that exists. I am one with everything, the same as everything—eternal, and not bound by my temporary physical self. I am those particles of light and I am the love and peace that I felt in that expansive moment of awakening. I've called this single unit of cosmic consciousness and cosmic energy "LifeParticles" to draw attention to this concept of who we really are.

LifeParticles and Quantum Physics

We know that all things are composed of tiny elementary particles. Here on earth, the land, water, and even the air around you can be broken down into subatomic particles. In fact, everything that physically exists in the universe is composed of these elementary particles that constantly vibrate at varying frequencies.

On the subatomic level, there is no difference between the fundamental substance that makes up your body and a distant, unknown planet in an unidentified galaxy. Everything in this universe is made up of the same "stuff." It just exists in different forms, shapes, and different energy patterns of vibration. LifeParticles is the name that I gave to this fundamental substance that makes up everything—including our very selves.

The worldview of quantum physics shares similar attributes with the LifeParticles that I experienced in that expansion of consciousness. Things appear to be solid and separate from one another on the level at which our physical senses normally perceive them. On a finer level, however, such as the atomic and subatomic levels, seemingly solid matter eventually turns out to be just pure energy. Modern science discovered that matter and energy are equivalent and interchangeable.

In the last century, some of the greatest scientific minds discovered that elementary particles can act as distinct particles, waves of energy, or both. More to the point, matter exists as waves of probabilities until it is observed. When observed by a conscious mind, these waves manifest into a physical reality.

We can infer from this experiment, and others, that the expectations and intentions of consciousness, as an observer, can affect the behavior of elementary particles. If our consciousness has an effect on how elementary particles act, then we are constantly affecting ourselves and the world around us with our consciousness, because everything is made of the same stuff.

In fact, we are always creating our reality, whether we are aware of it or not. Even though we can't always control the world as we want, and there are many other factors affecting what's happening in our lives, we know that our mind itself plays the most significant role. This is why the Buddhist *Flower Garland Sutra* says that "everything is created by the mind," and the Law of Attraction states that thoughts become things.

Eastern philosophy and medicine have long held the concept of life energy, called ki, chi, qi, or prana, depending on the culture. Western mystical traditions have also called the mysterious force that animates life by various names. My term, *LifeParticles*, is not that different, in essence, from this ancient knowledge of energy.

My intention behind this new term is to emphasize our true nature as an inseparable unity of energy and consciousness as well as the tremendous power we can receive from this awakening.

Ancient wisdom has told us for ages that energy arises from consciousness, and consciousness arises from energy; they are just different expressions of the same substance. Quantum physics also hints that mind and matter or subject and object are not separate. This may not be an easy concept to grasp at first. However, when you do LifeParticle Meditation, your experience will reveal to you that this is something we innately know, and it happens every moment in the very fabric of our lives. More importantly, if you apply that understanding to real-life situations, you will find that your opportunities for growth and freedom will have no limits.

If we view meditation from a practical perspective, the term *LifeParticles* provides a more tangible feeling than the word *energy*. Energy generally brings to mind the image of an elusive flow. When we hear the word *particles*, though, we are likely to visualize more concrete objects, such as grains of shining light. By using the concept of LifeParticles, my hope is that meditation will be more easily and widely accessible to more people. In addition, I aspire to the belief that LifeParticle Meditation can give us a more comprehensive experience of who we really are.

One thing that I will repeatedly stress throughout this book is the power of your consciousness. LifeParticles are the particles of consciousness, but at the same time, they respond to your conscious mind. LifeParticles exist as infinite potential until some information, idea, or intention is added to them. At that point, they are moved by that information, idea, or intention to create tangible objects and definite events based upon that information.

Through LifeParticles, the thoughts in your mind are the seeds of your present and future experiences that will blossom when given enough energy through action with your focused attention. Your thoughts also color your perspective, and thus influence how you experience LifeParticles in the form of the external and internal stimuli that come your way.

By understanding the principles behind how LifeParticles operate, and learning how to use them through LifeParticle Meditation, you can choose your thoughts and emotions and focus your mind on what is really meaningful and beneficial to you. Instead of being swayed by the random incidents and accidents of life, you can shape and direct your life in perfect sync with life itself. By realizing you are LifeParticles, that is, a being of consciousness and energy, and a mediator of mind and matter, you exercise your greatest strength—the ability to turn a possibility into a reality. In so doing, you create your experiences. You can be the miracle maker for your life.

chapter 2

Consciousness Creates Reality

Through the discoveries of modern physics, we have learned that conscious mind is involved in the manifestation of physical reality. However, there are many other interesting observations hinting that mind can influence the physical objects in our daily life.

The first one is our own body. In the 1950s, an English container ship that conveyed Portuguese Madeira wine anchored in a Scottish port to offload some cargo. One crewmember went into a refrigerated container to check whether all the cargo had been unloaded. While he was inside, another crewmember unknowingly closed and locked the door. The trapped crewmember used all his strength to pound on the walls, but to no avail. No one heard his cries, and the ship left for Portugal. When it arrived in Lisbon a few days later, the man was discovered dead inside the refrigerated container. Its walls contained a detailed record of the pain the man had suffered, which he wrote using a piece of metal. He had recorded how his body was slowly paralyzed and frozen by the frigid air and how the resultant injuries caused unbearable pain until he finally turned into a lump of ice. But that wasn't the real shocker. What was most surprising was that the temperature inside the container measured 66 degrees Fahrenheit (19 degrees Celsius). The refrigeration in that container had not been turned on at any point because it held no cargo. In addition, there was food in the container that the man could have eaten.

Why, then, did the crewmember freeze to death? Apparently, he believed with absolute certainty that he would freeze to death because he was in a refrigerated container, and his body followed his belief. It had nothing at all to do with his actual situation, that is, with whether the temperature of the room where he was trapped was actually below freezing. His imagination of his own death caused the result. If he had cast off his belief that he would freeze to death and had sought a way to sustain himself, he would have survived.

This account, from the book *Encyclopédie du Savoir Relatif et Absolu* [*Encyclopedia of Relative and Absolute Knowledge*], by French author Bernard Werber, clearly shows just how powerful are the operations of the brain. Your mind, and its many functions, is one of the most influential operations of the brain. What is amazing is that the brain is unable to distinguish between the mind's imagination and reality. Whatever your mind believes is real your brain then truly perceives and processes as real.

Dreaming is one of the functions that truly demonstrates this operation of the brain. For instance, have you ever had something sad happen in a dream and found yourself actually sobbing or shedding tears? Or have you ever broken out in a cold sweat or been shocked and awakened when something scary happened in a dream? Even though these are clearly illusions, in that moment, your brain completely believes they are real. In accordance with the information perceived by the brain, physiological manifestations appear in reality, such as your brain waves and respiration changing and your body shedding tears and sweating. This sort of thing happens quite often in everyday life—not just in dreams.

Merely imagining that you are meeting someone you love can cause your body to overflow with happy energy and bring a smile to your face; on the other hand, imagining that you are eating a slice of very sour lemon can fill your mouth with saliva and bring a grimace to your face. Just imagining these things, even though they haven't actually happened, causes your brain to react as if they had.

The Power of Perception

There was a psychologist and pharmacist in France named Émile Coué. Late one night, a patient arrived without a doctor's prescription, complaining of severe pain and asking for some medicine. Coué felt sorry for the person and, unable to bring himself to refuse, gave him a sugar pill that actually contained no medically active component. He told him that the medication would help and advised him to be sure to go to a hospital the next day. Coué met the person a few days later. The patient told him that he'd been completely healed after taking the medicine and hadn't needed to go to the hospital.

The medicine had no medically active components at all, so how could something like that happen? In his consciousness, the patient perceived it to be medicine that could eliminate his pain. With his trust in both the medicine and the pharmacist, he had no doubts at all. His belief directly affected his brain, to the extent that even this fake medicine had the same effect on his body as that of authentic medicine. Coué discovered then the phenomenon that would later become known as the "placebo effect."

The placebo effect is a pervasive phenomenon widely used in medical and pharmaceutical research and teaches us about the role of the brain and the importance of perception in health.

Dr. Herbert Benson of Harvard University Medical School called the placebo effect "remembered wellness" because it stems from the effects of the patient's expectations, including the patient's trust in the other person. Dr. Hunter "Patch" Adams, upon whom a movie was based, demonstrated that a patient's trust in their physician could improve their condition. Casting off a doctor's traditional stance of authority, "Patch" shares his friendship with patients and treats them as lifelong friends. He truly believes that "friendship is the best medicine" and that the state of mind that feels deep trust and friendship can cause the state of the body to recover.

There is also a phenomenon opposite to that of the placebo effect, wherein the body can actually deteriorate because of an expectation that it will deteriorate. This is called the "nocebo effect." In contrast with placebo, which is Latin for "I will please," nocebo means "I will harm." With the nocebo effect, your negative thoughts and mind-set, regardless of their validity, will also have a negative impact on your body.

An example of this is a fascinating experiment conducted by the Korean Broadcasting System for a TV documentary, in which an existing, ordinary brand of milk was advertised as a "newly developed diet milk" and tested at a beverage tasting event. The reactions of those who drank the milk were positive; in fact, many said that it tasted lighter and fresher than ordinary milk.

One of the participants, however, said she felt nauseous after drinking it, and another even vomited. Both were actually putting on a performance that was planned in advance with the producers. On seeing this, however, other tasters changed their initially positive reaction to a negative reaction, with comments such as "It tastes spoiled," and "I feel nauseous." Even more surprising was the fact that one of the tasters experienced itching all over her body that turned red as she developed a fever. She reportedly hurried to the hospital and received treatment. The doctor said she showed symptoms of food poisoning.

In fact, the milk used in the experiment was identical

with ordinary milk and had not spoiled at all. In this case, a simple change of information evolved beyond psychological discomfort to produce manifestations in the material world like vomiting, rashes, and hives. This clearly shows how powerfully information—and the mind—impacts the brain and body.

Coué viewed the human self as divided into conscious and unconscious elements, with will belonging to the conscious part and imagination belonging to the unconscious part. He observed that the problems of patients tended to increase when their conscious and unconscious minds, that is, their will and imagination, were in conflict with each other. This he called "self-conflict."

For example, the more patients tried to sleep, the more they ended up being awake. The more they tried to quit smoking, the more tobacco they ended up smoking. Given only the will to force oneself to sleep or quit smoking, he said, renders it impossible to fundamentally solve these problems.

Coué surmised that one should instead concentrate more on the power of the imagination and discard the will. In a confrontation between the will and imagination, the imaginative powers of the unconscious mind would always exhibit the greater strength, he said, adding that if the will and imagination were expressed in the same direction, their energy would have an effect several times greater. To align their will and imagination, Coué had people repeat at the start and end of their day, and also throughout their daily lives, the following optimistic autosuggestion:

"Day by day, in every way, I'm getting better and better."

Many of the studies and experiments of modern psychology demonstrate how the mind affects reality. A team led by Dr. Becca Levy of Yale University examined a database of people age fifty and older who responded to questions on what they thought of aging. Some people believed that health was bound to decline as one got older, while others thought that they could be healthy even as they aged.

This group had been followed for twenty-three years. When she looked at what happened to them, Dr. Levy made a surprising discovery—those with positive age stereotypes lived seven and a half years longer than those with negative stereotypes. People with positive age stereotypes were also more likely to eat a balanced diet, exercise, limit their alcohol consumption, stop smoking, and get regular physical exams. They had a higher level of physical functioning over time. In a similar study, individuals with a positive age stereotype were more likely to recover fully from a disability.

What do you think your old age will be like? When you think of your future, does healthy aging come to mind, or a picture of yourself in a state of debilitation? As we can see from the research mentioned above, your future will unfold according to the image you have in your mind right now. Amazing, isn't it? Even more amazing is that your present is a projection on reality of your inner landscape, which you have brought forward with you, whether consciously or unconsciously, from your past. The structure of the mind-set and consciousness you unwittingly embraced in the past was the blueprint that created who you are today.

Thoughts Influence Particles

As already indicated by the discoveries of modern physics, the influence of our own conscious mind doesn't seem to be limited to the scope of one's own body.

One experiment anyone can easily do to demonstrate how the mind affects reality is the Onion Experiment. Jinhee Kim, an elementary school teacher who does LifeParticle Meditation in South Korea, conducted this experiment with her students to show them the power of their thoughts and thus hopefully encourage them to improve their behavior. The children habitually cursed at each other, fought over trivial things, and, as a group, enjoyed shunning certain children as if it was a game. There was no end to the incidents and accidents occurring due to the children's thoughtless, coarse words and behavior.

Kim's method was simple. On each of three glasses filled with water, they placed an onion that had been grown under identical temperature, humidity, and lighting. However, they wrote down very different messages for each onion; whenever someone would look at one, he or she would read the message aloud. To the onion they named "Love Onion," they attached affirmative messages such as "I love you," "Thank you," and "I like you;" to the "Hate Onion," they attached negative messages such as "I hate you," "You irritate me," and "Die!" They attached no messages at all to the remaining "Disinterest Onion" and, in fact, no one paid it any attention.

The children actively took part in the project, and whenever

The left onion was told, "I love you," and the right onion, "I hate you." Your thoughts and energy influence everything around you.

they looked at the onions, really put their hearts into it. After about fifteen days of this, the onions had definitely grown in different ways. The Love Onion not only had healthy roots, but also had grown straight, and its shoots were green. The Hate Onion, though, had yellow shoots, and its roots had grown much less. The Disinterest Onion was even more surprising. Of the three onions, the Disinterest Onion had the slowest rate of growth; its shoots and roots had developed poorly, and it actually ended up rotting.

The reactions of the children who witnessed this experiment were impressive. As the saying goes, "seeing is believing." After confirming with their own eyes how great an impact their thoughts and words had on the real world, the children changed their behavior. Children who had habitually used foul language tried to speak kindly to, take a little more interest in, and become closer to their classmates—even those they didn't like. With this simple experiment, Kim enabled even young children to realize how great an impact the actions of the mind have on reality.

Another experiment reveals the mechanism behind the Onion Experiment. Dr. Masaru Emoto, who is researching water in Japan, wrote the words "Thank you" on a laboratory dish into which he had poured water. After freezing the water in a refrigeration chamber for three hours, photographs taken of the water's ice crystals revealed they were well-organized, clean, and hexagonal in shape. In contrast, the water in containers bearing words that roughly equated to "You make me sick" exhibited ice crystals that were randomly formed and distorted. Water in containers bearing the words "Please do that" exhibited well-formed crystals, while water in containers with the words "You can't do it!" failed to create crystals.

Through such experiments, Dr. Emoto says, it is possible to see that positive words like love and gratitude change matter and improve its quality, while negative words lead matter in a destructive direction, and that the words we use in our daily lives are very precious. In addition to words, Emoto also conducted experiments using music and images. For example, water exposed to Beethoven's *Pastoral Symphony* exhibited beautiful, well-formed crystals befitting the exhilarating melodies of the work, whereas water exposed to noisy music

A crystal of water when it was told "love" and "gratitude."

A crystal of water when it was told, "You make me sick."

full of angry language exhibited randomly formed crystals.

The conclusion he reached, after repeating these experiments, was that water creates beautiful hexagonal crystals in response to information—words, sounds, and images—that is life-giving and harmonious, but does not create crystals in response to contaminated information that runs counter to the flow of nature. This is because water accurately reflects the energy waves that carry information.

We all know that water does not possess a "brain," but is remarkably sensitive in its response to information. How much greater an influence, then, does information have on humans, who possess highly developed sensory, cognitive, and decision-making faculties? Moreover, the human body contains an average of forty to forty-five liters of water, which makes up 60 to 70 percent of a person's body weight. When we remember such facts, we cannot help but think deeply about how we have treated ourselves and other people—our attitudes, words, and actions—and about how we should treat them in the future.

Is it possible to change the effects of negative thoughts and words? What would happen if you sent healing information to contaminated water? Dr. Masaru Emoto states that, although the water won't be immediately affected, its water crystals will eventually change into beautiful forms if one continues to provide it with such information. Although negative thoughts, like those involved in resentment and disinterest, have a harmful, toxic effect on the blood, organs, and cells of the human body, your body and mind can be cured by thoughts—by LifeParticles of love—if you continue to send them with loving intention. This presents us with a great hope for healing.

By extending our understanding a little further, we can easily infer that your mind influences those around you, including your family, friends, and colleagues; their minds, in turn, also influence you. For example, let's say that you have an argument with a friend over something trivial. Later, you will probably remember something your friend said in the argument that hurt you, and you will fume with anger and resentment every time it occurs to you. It would be better if that angry mind-set remained only within you, but the mind is very agile. The moment you embrace such an attitude, it is conveyed immediately to your friend. The information "angry with your friend" would affect your friend and have a negative impact on his or her energy condition—and yours—as well as on your own body, on onions, water, and many other things.

You Are Creating Your Life in Every Moment

Since particles respond to the human mind, and everything is made of elementary particles, even nonliving objects are influenced by your thoughts.

For instance, consider the sense of the sacred and the calm and peace you feel when you go to a place where people meditate or pray. Often people will observe, "There is good energy here," when they visit such a spot. The sincere hearts of the people meditating and praying there have, over time, influenced the buildings, furniture, plants in the area, and even the particles in the air.

Wouldn't it be possible, then, for you to fill your own space with healthy and loving LifeParticles? Housecleaning removes dust and grime, but while you are giving your attention to your house, the contents of your mind are seeping into it. Clean with a positive mind to ensure that your house is filled with bright LifeParticles. This also applies to when you take a shower or prepare food or eat a meal. If you infuse your mind with positivity as you complete the task, waves of energy will change into positive particles and lead to good results.

For example, if you devote yourself fully to preparing a meal, it will be delicious, and you will feel the joy of those eating it. If you eat food that lacks devotion, on the other hand, you are bound to get the feeling that something is missing. If you pour your heart into making a meal, that mind-set goes into the energy of the food and the elementary particles of which it is made. In the same way, if you lack a devoted heart, your food will have that much less flavor and quality.

This correlates with Asian methods of spiritual cultivation commonly called "cultivating the mind." According to these traditions, wherever the mind focuses, it affects elementary particles, and the results manifest in reality. Thus, the heart of spiritual training is cultivating the "field of the mind" by watching the mind, the foundation of all things, and obtaining answers from the mind.

Each and every moment of your life is an instant of creation that causes LifeParticles to move. Therefore, whether you are walking or standing, sitting or lying down, speaking or silent, active or still, do not neglect a single moment. Each moment is an opportunity to put a mind full of sincerity into all of your thoughts and actions.

Do you dream of change in your life? Do you want to live a healthier, happier life? If so, then look into the garden of your heart. See what weeds are growing thickly, and where, and boldly pull them out. Have the weeds, perhaps, grown rampant in your garden while its master showed no interest, thus preventing its flowers from blooming beautifully and its trees from bearing fruit? Those weeds are the emotions or attachments to which you cling. They are the feelings of inferiority or inadequacy that have made you feel small and insignificant, or the walls of preconception that have separated you from others.

Those who are able to watch over and beautifully tend the gardens of their minds, and those who are able to use the power of their potent minds, are the creators of life. Don't wait for some other person or thing to make your life beautiful. Become the artist of your own life.

Your mind creates everything. Your conscious mind has much greater power than you can ever imagine. Your mind can create blessings or disasters, can heal or harm, can bring abundance or absence. It is up to your mind whether the world looks hopeful or hopeless.

Awaken to the power of your mind. That power will cause LifeParticles to move. Your mind guides LifeParticles in the vast terrain of unlimited possibilities. LifeParticle Meditation is all about exercising the power of our own mind.

chapter 3

Open Your MindScreen

As I've told people about the concept of LifeParticles, I've also spoken about another concept—its partner, so to speak. I call it the "MindScreen." The MindScreen is a space and channel through which LifeParticles move and are active and the space of consciousness where all of your mental activities take place. I've visualized, and turned into a kind of space, the mental activity we call "mind" and "consciousness" using the concrete idea of a MindScreen.

By associating it with the word screen, people assume that the MindScreen is a kind of plane, like a projection screen. The MindScreen, however, is a multidimensional space not subject to the restrictions of space and time. Through the MindScreen, you can transcend space and time to engage in infinite creation. Everyone has a MindScreen. This is because human beings have a high-performance computer—the brain.

Why don't you test your MindScreen right now? Try bringing to mind the face of the friend you want to see most. What image do you see? Although it's fine to close your eyes, that friend's face will come to mind even if you keep your eyes open. Now try to visualize, one by one, the details of your friend's face—his or her eyes, nose, mouth, and hair. Isn't that friend smiling at you?

The space of consciousness that I call the "MindScreen" has just spread out before you due to the action of your brain. This is not a space you can touch with your hands, though. If you concentrate, it appears like a hologram in empty space, and then scatters immediately unless you focus your awareness. The MindScreen is the brain's magic trick that causes LifeParticles to come together and then scatter.

I say that your brain contains a high-performance video camera, video editor, and projector. Your video camera records what you see and hear every day, whether or not you are aware of it. And your video editor edits for you the things you've imaged. From the recording, it keeps some part for your conscious memory and other parts in storage for future reference, or releases them into oblivion. Even during sleep, when your consciousness is taking a break, your brain assigns meaning to the day's experiences and converts short-term memories into long-term memories. And this is not all. It also creates new images, called "dreams," and projects them on your MindScreen.

When you are awake, as well as when you are asleep, the

projector continues to cast images on your MindScreen. Your MindScreen operates continuously—when you bring to mind things from your past, when you imagine something, when you are lost in thought, and even when you are lost in fantasy. For instance, if you are in love, the face of your beloved will flicker before your eyes even while you are eating or reading a book; if you are obsessed with billiards, then colored balls will roll around on the ceiling while you are lying in your bed. Your body is in the physical world, but your mind is active in a different world of consciousness that is, through your MindScreen, as if you are looking at your lover's face or holding a cue in a pool hall.

MindScreen—The Brain's Latent Function

What would happen if you more deliberately used your brain's functions for recording, editing, and projecting in this way? If you haven't been using these brain functions consciously, or if you aren't using them properly, then your brain is like a video camera, video editor, and video projector without an owner.

These apparatuses, in fact, perform their functions very faithfully for you even though you don't try to operate them, and even though you, their owner, show no interest in them. The problem, however, is that those devices are repeating only the very simple, basic functions originally set to run automatically. Their advanced functions are not utilized because their owner shows little interest in them; thus, that is all they can do. If you only use your brain's simple, basic functions, then it's like buying the newest, most advanced computer and using it only as a word processor. However, you can't use your brain's advanced functions unless you know how.

In Korea, there are many students who use MindScreen and LifeParticle Meditation for their learning and study. During class, they record what their teacher is saying—just as if they were taking a video with a camera. They not only focus on the teacher's explanations but also, conscious of their brains, imagine themselves shooting a video of their teacher's lecture and recording the data in their own brains. Later, whenever they have time, often during their breaks between classes, they call up the scenes they had recorded on their MindScreen, and then replay and edit them to make them easier to remember.

Before working on the MindScreen, they often do simple exercises to relax the body and mind and create a pleasant state for the brain. A relaxed and pleasant state allows the MindScreen to be fully functional. One of the frequently used relaxation methods is Brain Wave Vibration; this involves simply shaking the head gently from side to side. The students have said that doing this exercise for a few moments helps them feel refreshed and puts their mind at ease; it's as if distracting thoughts and worries are shaken out of the brain.

After preparing the body, mind, and brain in this way, they open the MindScreen and display on it those scenes they want to edit. As they play their recording of class from beginning to end, they cut out unneeded scenes and underline in red or edit the content on their screen that their teacher stressed was important. They summarize the key points of the lesson using their MindScreen, just as people do when organizing their notes on paper. If they later review the film of their memory they've edited in this way, it's much easier to recall what they have studied. With this MindScreen learning method, many of them have significantly improved their grades.

These examples teach us that the potential of the human brain has no boundaries. Do you doubt that you could use the MindScreen in this way because it seems so advanced? These students are not special children who have always had such faculties. Anyone can develop this kind of skill with consistent practice. Learning and study is not the only area in which you can use MindScreen; MindScreen, combined with the power of LifeParticles, greatly assists you in improving every aspect of your life.

Using Your MindScreen

MindScreen is a spatial representation of your consciousness. When you perceive your consciousness, it can be viewed as a vast space that I call MindScreen. Opening your MindScreen means exercising your consciousness. In a sense, you are using your MindScreen all the time, whether you are aware of it or not. However, when you consciously use it, it can truly make a difference in your life.

Try the following methods and see how Mind-Screen works for you. The time that is best for using your

MindScreen is in the morning, when you begin your day. After some relaxing exercises, sit comfortably on the floor or on a chair. Close your eyes and turn on your MindScreen. Turning on your MindScreen means that you are projecting a vast visual plane in your mind's eye. Imagine bright LifeParticles illuminating your MindScreen. Now, on your screen, display the important things you need to achieve today. You may get ideas and inspirations about what you have to do. When you bring up the faces of the people you will meet that day, try sending them bright LifeParticles. Images and insights about what you should say to them and how you should treat them could very well come to mind at this time.

Turn on your MindScreen whenever you wish to create something you want, not just during such morning meditations. If there is something you want—health, happiness, improved relationships, changed habits, material abundance, achievement, or whatever—display it on your MindScreen, and then imagine it being achieved successfully. For example, if you have a job, try turning on your MindScreen and rehearsing an upcoming meeting or presentation.

All great imaginative minds and visionaries throughout history have been adept at using the MindScreen. It is said that the world-famous speaker President John F. Kennedy would always give a speech in his imagination before going to sleep on the night prior to a planned public address. He would rehearse his speech as he imagined himself standing on stage. In fact, he would imagine the crowds cheering, and even the gestures, expressions, and tone of voice he should adopt, as concrete reality.

Many athletes use the method of visualizing their performance in their imagination, which means they display images on their MindScreen. American Olympic swimmer Michael Phelps, who in 2012 became the first person in history to win nineteen Olympic medals, fifteen of which were gold, is known for his use of mental visualization. Since he was seven years old, Phelps has been mentally relaxing his body and then watching what he calls his "videotape" of the perfect swim in his mind each night before he goes to sleep.

In his book *Beneath the Surface* Phelps wrote, "When I'm about to fall asleep, I visualize to the point that I know exactly what I want to do: dive, glide, stroke, flip, reach the wall, hit the split time to the hundredth, then swim back again for as many times as I need to finish the race." In one interview, he said, "I'm trying to picture it all, everything I possibly can, so that I'm ready for anything that happens." Rehearsing all possible scenarios in his mind helped Phelps in the final of the 200-yard butterfly event at the Beijing Olympics in 2008. When his goggles filled with water and he had to swim blind, Michael kept calm and broke his world record in this event, because he had already practiced for this roadblock many times in his mind.

Eunju Jeong, a college lecturer, restored her relationship with her daughter through her MindScreen. Her daughter, Hayeon, who is in her second year of high school, had such a weak constitution that she barely weighed eighty-eight pounds. She had been to the doctor's office frequently since she was young because of rhinitis, allergic conjunctivitis, allergic eczema, stress-induced nephritis, and other ailments. Eunju was slowly being worn down by endlessly tending to her daughter. She also had other children, a husband, and a career to look after. In the middle of lecturing, she would have to rush home without delay after receiving a phone call that Hayeon was ill, and always flustered and in a hurry, she would have to follow her daughter home, to school, and to the hospital, and then return to work. On such days, she would arrive home in the evening and lose control, thinking, is this living?

Completely exhausted, Eunju got to the point where she just gave up on Hayeon's health problems. She thought, I did what I could. What more can I do? When it's time for her to get better, she'll get better on her own. She grew indifferent toward her daughter, without even realizing it, and was irritable in the way she treated and spoke to her. Confused by her mother's attitude, Hayeon would hide in her room. Seeing this, Eunju would think, oh, no! and regret her behavior; however, in such moments, it was already too late. Her relationship with Hayeon quickly cooled as such incidents were repeated, and it became hard for Eunju to control herself.

With both body and mind completely drained by her job, housework, and caring for her sick daughter, Eunju realized that she should get her own act together first, and started LifeParticle Meditation. One day, she was doing LifeParticle Meditation at home when she suddenly thought, if I give up on Hayeon, she might never get better. She might have to live her whole life like that. I want to see Hayeon cheerful and happy. The moment she thought that, Eunju was overwhelmed with sorrow and remorse for how she had treated her daughter.

Pulling her mind together, she brought up her MindScreen and visualized Hayeon. As always, Hayeon looked weak and languid. With devotion and concentration, Eunju imagined LifeParticles, sparkling bits of elementary particles, flowing to her daughter. She imagined filling her hands with golden energy and using them to sweep across every part of Hayeon's body. The more she did this, the brighter her daughter's expression grew until she was smiling cheerfully, surrounded by golden light. When Eunju saw this, tears streamed unbidden from her eyes.

"I'm sorry. I'm sorry! I feel really sorry for how I've treated you. I love you, my beautiful daughter, Hayeon! I truly love you," Eunju told her in her mind.

After her meditation, Eunju went to her daughter's room and gave her sleeping daughter a warm hug. As if she had felt something even in her sleep, Hayeon leaned against her mother and said, "Hold me like this, Mom, for just five minutes." Eunju held her tightly and thought, as they travel around every nook and cranny of your body, LifeParticles will heal all your hurts.

Eunju changed after that, becoming very gentle in her attitude and words toward her daughter. The awkwardness and iciness in their relationship melted away like spring snow.

You can bring anything, anyone, or any situation to your MindScreen and nurture your intentions by sending it LifeParticles. Your MindScreen, a 360-degree hologram, is a place to make your visualization more tangible with the great assistance of LifeParticles. Your MindScreen hosts and channels LifeParticles wherever and to whatever your mind directs them. Remember, you are a great magician capable of creating miracles by sprinkling LifeParticles on your MindScreen.

• • •

When you open your mind,
it can cover the universe.
When you close your mind,
it will become smaller than the smallest pinprick.

• • •

chapter 4

Recover Your Zero Point

The MindScreen is an operation of consciousness arising from the brain. To turn on your MindScreen, though, you need to learn a few basic things about your brain.

For your MindScreen to operate well, your brain must be in a "pleasant" state. A "pleasant brain state" means that distracting thoughts have quieted and energy circulates well in your brain, enhancing brain functions like concentration, imagination, and creativity.

Our brain transmits its own special brand of energy, called brain waves, which are associated with various states of consciousness. They are the flow of electricity that is generated when signals are transmitted between your brain cells. The brain waves we see when most people are awake and go about their everyday activities are rapidly moving beta waves, which have a frequency of 13-30 Hz. These appear often in the front part of the brain when we speak, when we engage in conscious activities like moving, when we are tense or excited, when we engage in complicated thoughts and calculations, and when we worry. If our bodies and minds relax and become more comfortable, our brain waves will slow down to alpha waves (8-12 Hz). These appear mostly at the top and back part of the brain.

If you enter a deeper state of meditation, the waves become even slower, and theta waves (4-8 Hz) are generated. When your brain produces theta waves, your awareness rests somewhere between the conscious and unconscious layers of your mind. In that state, your cognitive abilities improve; you exhibit outstanding physical performance; you can experience deep insight; and you may have a burst of creative thought or problem-solving ability. Theta brain waves are seen in people who, after struggling for a long time with a difficult problem, suddenly get a creative solution or inspiration. Superior athletes are said to achieve an almost meditative state free of thought during competition; this state, often called "the zone," emphasizes and strengthens their focus. Anxiety, pain, fear of failure—all such thoughts disappear, leaving only a sense of clarity and joy.

The conscious world is like the tip of a massive iceberg that can be easily seen above the ocean's surface. The unconscious world, on the other hand, is akin to the rest of the iceberg hidden below the water. The clarity and focus experienced when your brain is in a deep meditative state allows you to see down into the ocean of your mind and explore your unconscious. It's the ideal brain state for using your MindScreen, which forms a bridge or channel connecting your conscious mind and unconscious mind. This state makes your visualization and imagination work more effectively for your conscious goals and dreams. Once you open your MindScreen and enter a deep, meditative state, you will discover the world of the unconscious spreading out before you and find yourself surrounded by the light of LifeParticles.

The brains of longtime meditators produce theta waves throughout the day, even when they are not sitting in full meditation; they are able to maintain a theta state at will. In the same way, if you can maintain your brain in a pleasant state through repeated practice, you will be able to keep your MindScreen open in your daily life—not only when you sit and meditate. If you are always actively using your MindScreen, then you will see the world through your MindScreen and be able to create what you desire more successfully. Then, meditation becomes your life, and your life becomes meditation.

Wake Up Your Life Brain

In this meditative state, you become so hyperaware you can even sense the inside of your body. You can feel the location of your different organs, even your brain, and have a sense of their activity. For instance, you may be able to detect the energy circulation in your brain by sensing that one area is fluid while another is relatively inactive. With this kind of awareness, you can activate the energy circulation in your brain or calm down your brain waves with just your attention.

The brain plays a central role in human consciousness and is crucial for human life. While we haven't yet discovered everything there is to know about the brain, humanity has made great strides over the last century in unraveling its complexities.

One psychological model, proposed by the American physician and neuroscientist Paul D. MacLean, simplifies how we can look at the brain by dividing it into three layers: the neocortex, the limbic system, and the central core. I have found this evolutionary triune brain theory useful for describing and observing the brain and its activities, especially as related to meditation.

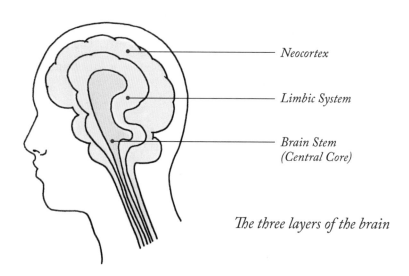

Neocortex

Limbic System

Brain Stem
(Central Core)

The three layers of the brain

The neocortex is the outermost part of the cerebrum and the most recent part of the brain to evolve. The human neocortex is more than ten times larger relative to body weight than that of a dog or cat. Development of the neocortex is an important characteristic that distinguishes humans from other animals. Brain activity that is unique to humans—using language and analyzing, integrating, and evaluating information—takes place here. That is why the neocortex is also called the "Rational Brain" or "Thinking Brain." In our day-to-day lives, the analyzing and judging activities of our neocortex can become dominant and suppress the areas of the brain that take care of our emotional stability and physical vitality.

Operations related to emotions are handled by the limbic system, which is located below the neocortex. The limbic system developed in what is often called the mammalian stage of evolution, and is involved in a variety of functions, such as emotional states, motivation, and memory formation. The limbic system is known as the "Emotional Brain" or "Feeling Brain."

The bottom layer of the brain is the central core. It includes the brain stem and cerebellum, and appeared in the reptilian stage of evolution. The brain stem regulates the essential vital functions, including respiration, heartbeat, blood pressure, and digestion, and the cerebellum plays a major role in balance and movement. Although influenced by the neocortex, the central core can operate independently of it. You breathe, your heart beats, and you digest your food without even worrying about it all, thanks to your brain stem. Thus, the brain stem can be called the "Life Brain" or the "Unconscious Brain" in the sense that your conscious mind doesn't have direct access to it.

We don't know exactly where the unconscious mind is located, but the power of the unconscious mind is recognized in many ways. The unconscious mind can create physical and emotional states that are unconnected to your conscious thought processes. This has been shown through hypnosis, through which you can bypass the conscious mind and access the unconscious. For example, if you put someone into a deep, hypnotic state and suggest, "I'm placing a very hot coin in the palm of your hand," and then put a regular quarter in the palm of the person's hand, a burn mark can appear there.

Trained meditators experience an eruption inside their brain when their minds are in a deep meditative state. This eruption is reflected in our brain waves. It occurs when your brain waves reach a theta frequency. In this state of mind, the activity of the brain stem increases dramatically as the thoughts and emotions of the neocortex and the limbic system are reduced. This, then, is the calm and clear state that integrates the three layers of your brain, and thus allows your body's natural healing processes or creative inspiration to emerge from the world of the unconscious through the MindScreen.

The team of Dr. Herbert Benson of Harvard University Medical School demonstrated a similar pattern of brain activity through functional MRI (fMRI) imaging. He showed that when a person meditates, two psychologically contradictory phenomena occur simultaneously: stability and agitation. He called this the "paradox of calm commotion." In his experiments, even though the overall activity of the brain became quieter during meditation, activity increased in those sections of the brain, such as the brain stem, associated with autonomic regulation of blood pressure, heart rate, and respiration. Activity also increased in regions linked to attention, awareness of space-time concepts, and executive control of decision-making. We can assume this activity was connected with the sense of space and the increased concentration and insight that people experience when they enter meditative states.

Dr. Benson said, "I can be confident that any outward or conscious activity and thoughts I may be watching are merely the tip of a vast brain-body iceberg, which is supporting the unfolding peak experience."

Creation Occurs in a State of Nothingness

What is this vast, hidden iceberg of the unconscious, and what happens if we access an unconscious state?

What I encountered in my brain through meditation, when my thoughts and emotions quieted and I went to the very bottom of my consciousness, was empty space that spread out in all directions. I found myself in the center of that space that I could observe all around me. The deeper I went, the wider and more extensively that space expanded. I call this space a "nothingness" that anyone can find deep in their unconscious mind.

Physics also shows us how, when we look deep down in

the material world, we find empty space. If we expanded an atom to the size of a theater, its nucleus would be the size of a grain of dust at its center, and virtually invisible. Everything in the atom, except for the nucleus, is completely empty space, with just a few electrons moving and vibrating rapidly within it. If we go one step further, to below the level of the atom, all we find are vibrating waves within more empty space. If the atoms that make up our bodies and other matter are ultimately empty space, then our bodies are also, in the end, empty space, or nothingness.

That state of nothingness, however, is not actually where nothing exists. In fact, physicists say that even when the absolute temperature in a perfect vacuum is zero, and we would expect there to be no energy left, there is always some energy remaining in the elementary particles that make up all matter. They call that energy "zero-point energy," which is inherently present in the lowest possible energy state or the vacuum state.

Max Planck, winner of the Nobel Prize in Physics and one of the main originators of quantum physics, said, "All matter originates and exists only by virtue of a force which brings the particle of an atom to vibration and holds this most minute solar system of the atom together. We must assume behind this force the existence of a conscious and intelligent mind. This mind is the matrix of all matter."

Physicist Dr. Ervin Laszlo defined this zero-point field full of elementary particles as a sea of infinite potential and said, "The evolution of the living world is part of the great wave that created particles from the underlying virtual-energy and information field [that is] misleadingly called a vacuum."

This field of infinite potential energy that surrounds us is the nothingness we can experience through LifeParticle Meditation. The inherent energy of LifeParticles is neutral and pure. LifeParticles in a neutral state can be changed into anything at all—all it takes is the application of information from your consciousness. If you access this field of nothingness by going deep into your unconscious mind, you can connect your thoughts with the potential energy of this vast vacuum so that your thoughts can manifest in physical reality.

Thus, nothingness is like a pure, blank slate—a space of infinite creation on which you can draw anything. If you want to become healthier, and you project onto your MindScreen images of yourself in a healthier state, LifeParticles will act according to those images. If you want to become happier, and you project onto your MindScreen a vision of yourself as happy, LifeParticles will respond by creating the energy of happiness, and you will actually feel happier.

Buddhism uses the expression "Emptiness is form; form is emptiness," which means that form (phenomena) comes from emptiness (nothingness), and that form is, ultimately, complete nothingness, or emptiness. Another expression, "True emptiness and marvelous existence," means that being appears marvelously from a state of true void.

The world-class theoretical physicist David Bohm explained, "Just as the vast 'sea' of energy in space is present to our perception as a sense of emptiness or nothingness, so the vast 'unconscious' background of explicit consciousness with all its implications is present in a similar way. That is to say, it may be sensed as an emptiness, a nothingness, within which the usual content of consciousness is only a vanishingly small set of facets."

Have you ever had a great idea come to you, seemingly out of nowhere, when you've been intently thinking about a problem? It might feel like it came from some source outside of you, rather than from information you already knew you possessed. Perhaps it even came to you in a dream.

J. K. Rowling, the author who caused the worldwide Harry Potter craze, said, "The idea for Harry Potter simply fell into my head," while she was on a busy train traveling from Manchester to London. And it's not just her. Many authors and artists of great genius say that they were able to create their wonderful works when, at some instant, they were struck by amazing inspiration. Famous inventors and scientists also say they have had creative ideas instantaneously at the end of long, intense periods of concentration.

Our unconscious mind is tuned in to the information that exists in the vast universe. When we really want something or want to know something, it acts as an information magnet, automatically pulling that information to us until we become conscious of it.

If we bring our mind into a meditative state and open our MindScreen, we can find that information more easily and proactively from an unlimited source. In this way, we can use LifeParticles and our MindScreen to find answers to our questions and receive new, creative ideas.

Recover the Zero Point

"I heard talk about the Law of Attraction, that thoughts become things, and I got excited. So I kept imagining what I wanted. But nothing changed as a result."

There are people with complaints such as this who say that nothing happens no matter how much they imagine it. For instance, some don't lose weight even though they continue imagining losing weight, some remain depressed even though they imagine becoming happy, and some remain in poverty even though they imagine becoming materially wealthy ... have you, too, had a similar experience? Have you attempted it a few times, failed, and then given up, thinking, The Law of Attraction doesn't seem to apply to me?

Concepts that should apply universally are expressed as "laws" and "principles." If reality doesn't change according to your desires, then what in the world is the problem? The reason, I say, is this: It's because you desired something without recovering your zero point.

A state of consciousness of nothing, in which thought and emotion have quieted, I describe as the "zero point." And purifying those thoughts and emotions and entering that state of consciousness I describe as "recovering the zero point." Recovering the zero point is entering a neutral state of consciousness that doesn't lean in any direction at all. It is like having to pass through neutral when changing gears in a car. Once you have entered a pure, neutral state, genuine change and creation become possible through maximized concentration and brainpower and an unbiased and unobstructed consciousness.

The biggest reason things don't change, even though you imagine what you want, is that thoughts and emotions arising out of your long-established preconceptions and habits keep dragging you in some direction other than the one you want to go. If you truly want to change, you have to press a reset button capable of putting your thoughts and feelings to sleep and come back to a neutral state. Pressing the reset button of consciousness means "recovering your zero point."

LifeParticle Meditation is a very effective method for recovering your zero point. Through LifeParticle Meditation, if you enter a state of pure consciousness, you'll be freed from obsession with thoughts and emotions that jerk you around, and you'll finally gain the power to choose and create something new. You have to let go of whatever you hold in your hands if you choose to hold something new. In the same way, genuine choice and change finally become possible in a pure state that is emptied of thoughts and emotions.

To create the movie *Change: The LifeParticle Effect*, we held a workshop in September 2012 and invited people with no information about LifeParticles to come and experience LifeParticles for themselves. One participant, Rob DeSimone from New York, described his reason for participating in the workshop as follows:

"It is a long journey to actually get what I want. I want to find out what is inside of here [pointing to his heart]. I want to know about me. I honestly want to know, why am I here.

What does my soul want?"

Entering his internal consciousness through the workshop, and purifying emotional energy that had arisen from memories of the past, Rob later shared this:

"I'm going deep inside and learning a little more about myself. I think I was not only speaking to the present me, but [to the me] when I was small and my parents got divorced—I *loved* that kid. That kid was the perfect child, I mean, a good, loving kid, and I think that, as I got older, and [became affected by] different outside influences, I got a little bit more cynical to the point that I have all of this baggage . . . I think I have a much better idea of what I want, what makes me happy. The LifeParticles and the instructors definitely gave us tools to move forward, so now I can reach my goals, reach new heights, and become a better person."

If you earnestly desire to achieve something, begin with recovering your zero point by first entering your internal consciousness. Then, what you genuinely want will come up on your MindScreen, and you will be able to create a detailed plan on it very clearly; however, this can only happen when you achieve a pure state of consciousness—one that is like a blank slate on which you can draw anything. You will experience the truth that what your thoughts want, what your emotions want, and what your zero-point consciousness wants may each be very different.

Develop the habit of choosing from zero-point consciousness, no matter what your circumstances. When you choose what is wanted by the thoughts and emotions that originate in the desires of your ego, it's not easy to turn them into reality—for the power of true creation arises out of zero-point consciousness. If what you choose from zero-point consciousness is different from what your thoughts or emotions want, how can you attract and use the pure, intense power that comes out of zero-point consciousness to achieve what your desires want?

If the longing for something you want exists at the level of thought or at the level of emotion, then your consciousness has failed to enter deep into your unconscious mind and remains trapped in your Thinking Brain or Emotional Brain. At this level, no matter how much you may pray for the manifestation of what you want, your consciousness lingers where it is, fenced in by thought and emotion.

The miracles you want can never happen at the level of thought or emotion because miracles such as healing are a phenomenon of life. Just as the beating of your heart is not produced by your thoughts or emotions, so are miracles and all the great stories manifest in the world of life emptied of thought and emotion. When you completely empty your mind, your consciousness accesses the zero point, and you become able to activate the world of life as you wish.

If you are now dreaming of change, recover your zero point and discover what you want in pure, zero-point consciousness, unobstructed by thought and emotion. Particles of infinite potential that are always ready to change into anything will welcome you brightly.

• • •

You can encounter the great life within you
when you recover the zero point.
When you encounter that great life,
all limits created by the thoughts and emotions vanish
and infinite creativity springs forth.

• • •

chapter 5

Activate Your Energy System

The amazing outcomes caused by LifeParticles occur in the world of life, not by thoughts and emotions. To access the world of life, you have to quiet your thoughts and emotions and allow your consciousness to enter the zero point. What should you do, then, to quiet your thoughts and emotions?

As you may have experienced yourself, thoughts call up even more thoughts, and emotions bring up even more emotions. Thus, you cannot eliminate thoughts using thoughts or emotions using emotions. It's difficult to enter the world of life using the information—the general knowledge, experience, and memories—that you have been accumulating. From a certain perspective, such reasoning, knowledge, and past information could actually hinder your access to the world of life.

The way to quiet the humming of thoughts and emotions

in the neocortex and limbic systems is to focus on the actual vital activity inside your body. Focus on how your body feels for a while, and you will be able to sense life energy. Enter your mind riding on the waves and rhythms of that energy and the gates of the world of life will open before you.

To experience this process, you first need to understand the basic system and principles of the flow and operation of the energy circulating in your body.

In the East, people have long believed that life energy flows in all things in the universe. They have studied this energy over thousands of years, and have deduced a set of rules and principles by which this life energy operates. If you understand the systematic principles of energy in the human body that have long been used to good effect, you will be better able to understand and apply LifeParticles.

As I have been teaching countless people over the last thirty years, I have been researching through them the energy principles that govern the human body and consciousness. In that process, I gained a deeper understanding of how these principles work and felt great hope that we could solve many problems that humanity confronts. The keys I've discovered are:

1. Our body's energy system is inherently perfect.
2. There are specific principles of energy that govern our energy system.
3. The different physical and spiritual problems confronting us develop because the perfect operation of our energy system becomes impaired.

4. All of the problems confronting us can be solved if we can just restore that energy system to its original, healthy state. According to the principles of energy, this means that the energy in our bodies must circulate well. It doesn't matter whether those problems involve health, happiness, peace, or even enlightenment.

I've divided my explanation about these keys into two aspects that reflect different cultural and philosophical histories: energy pathways and energy centers. However, both are helpful and operate in conjunction with each other.

Meridians, the Energy Pathways

In addition to blood vessels and lymph vessels, our bodies have pathways, or "meridians," through which energy flows. This energy system is the basis of the traditional medicine that originated in China, Korea, and Japan. It describes twenty meridians that include twelve regular meridians, which are associated with twelve organs; and eight extraordinary meridians, which supplement the twelve regular meridians, although they are not directly related to organs.

Out of the twenty meridians, fourteen are usually involved in practices such as yoga, tai chi, qigong, and energy healing; these are the twelve regular meridians and two of the eight extraordinary meridians. One of these two extraordinary meridians flows along a central line at the front of the body, and the other flows along a central line at the back.

Meridian points located on these meridians are used in acupuncture and acupressure. If we compare meridians to railroad tracks along which trains of energy flow, then meridian points are like stations where the trains stop. People enter and exit trains at stations. Similarly, energy enters and exits the body at meridian points. About 365 major meridian points are generally known. As a year is divided into twelve months and 365 days, the twelve regular meridians and 365 major meridian points are often compared to these units of time.

This energy system is closely related to hormone secretion, and is also connected with each of the body's organs. For example, each of twelve organs has a corresponding meridian and energy points. In Eastern medicine, the application of acupuncture, moxibustion, acupressure, or energy healing to the corresponding meridians and points treats problems in those organs.

Chakras, the Energy Centers

Chakras are energy centers where the body's life energy is concentrated. The concept of chakra is found in the Hindu tradition in India and some disciplines of Buddhism. Of the seven major chakras, six are located along the spinal cord, and one is located at the crown of the head. The chakras are closely related to the endocrine system, which secretes hormones, and they are known to influence each and every part of the human body through the autonomic nervous system. They are highly attuned sensors that respond to the state of your physical, mental, and spiritual health.

The seven chakras are like a ladder whose steps denote the developmental stages of energy, body, and consciousness. For instance, the farther down the ladder you go, the more your physical aspects are influenced; and the farther up the ladder you go, the more your spiritual aspects are influenced. This does not mean, however, that the chakras at the bottom are unimportant. To activate the chakras above, the chakras below must first be activated.

You don't need to worry about learning all of the attributes and detailed information of each chakra. Knowing the approximate location of each chakra will be sufficient to experience benefits from LifeParticle Meditation. Let's look at some basic information about each chakra.

The first chakra and second chakra govern energy related to the body, physical vitality, reproduction, and sex, and, along with the third chakra, play a central role in your physical self. The color of deep red, the first chakra, also known as the root chakra, is located at the base of the spine. When the first chakra is activated, hot energy from it rises along the spinal cord to fill the second chakra.

The second chakra is located in the sacrum. An easy way to feel its energy is by concentrating on the core of your lower abdomen. It is the physical and energetic center of your body and your center of balance. This chakra, also known as the sacral chakra, is reddish-orange in color and the furnace of the energy system. If your lower abdomen is warm and full of energy, then you know that energy is circulating healthfully in your whole body.

The life energy of the second chakra rises along your spine to your third chakra; this orange-colored chakra is located at the level of the solar plexus, which is why it is also known as the solar plexus chakra.

When energy from your third chakra rises into your fourth chakra, which lies at the height of the center of your chest, the energy is purified. Your fourth chakra is your heart chakra. Many traditions visualize the heart chakra as a green color. In my personal experience, however, I've felt this chakra expresses a golden yellow color.

As the energy in the fourth chakra grows and becomes lighter and brighter, it naturally rises to the fifth chakra, in the throat, almost like water rising when it becomes vapor. This chakra, also known as the throat chakra, is a blue-green color, and acts like a filter to further purify the energy passing through it.

The sixth chakra is found at the top of the brain stem. This indigo-colored chakra is also called the brow chakra, or third eye, because an activated sixth chakra allows us to see the infinite wisdom of the universe. The activation of your sixth chakra opens your third eye, and you become able to experience a mystical cosmic light and energy entering your brain.

The seventh chakra, at the top of the head, is a major point through which energy enters the body, especially during LifeParticle Meditation. Also known as the crown chakra, this violet-colored chakra relates to our spiritual journey. When fully open and activated, the seventh chakra enables us to access the highest level of consciousness and oneness with all that exists.

Our chakras are healthy when they are open, strong, full of energy, and balanced, which means that all chakras are harmoniously activated and without blockage. People who are physically lethargic, who tire easily, who have weakened resistance to stress, or who have trouble controlling their emotions, have one or more chakras that are weak and/or low on energy. In this state, their environment can easily influence them. In contrast, people who have their chakras fully charged, strong, and balanced, are stable in body and mind and feel like sturdy pillars unshaken by their surroundings.

The process of activating all of your chakras, from the first through the seventh, through the accumulation of pure life energy is not something special that is possible only for certain individuals. Anyone can develop their body's energy system if they understand the principles by which it operates and practice exercises to open, activate, balance, and strengthen it. LifeParticle Meditation is a very simple, effective way of achieving that goal.

Energy Follows Where the Mind Goes

The most basic energy principle says that the power of the mind changes energy and matter. In Korean, we call it Shim

Ki Hyul Jung, which translates to "Energy Follows Where the Mind Goes." We already know that everything exists as energy—cosmic spaces, space and time, mind and body, even thought and consciousness all exist as energy. Because they are made of the same stuff, changes in one expression of energy will affect others, such as the mind affecting the body. For instance, with your mind, you can pull the energy that fills the universe into your individual being. That energy manifests differently, according to your intention and how powerfully you amplify it with your concentration.

The principle of Energy Follows Where the Mind Goes can be compared to the process of concentrating light with a magnifying glass. Light is scattered when you move a magnifying glass around. However, if you fix the magnifying glass in place and focus it precisely, the light energy collects and quickly becomes strong enough to start a fire. Our thoughts are like light. Scattered, dispersed thoughts have weak energy, but when they are concentrated in one place, they become powerful enough to create something.

With the power of your mind, you can freely control the energy in your body. You can send LifeParticles at will to your internal organs and other bodily tissues, and you can make certain parts of your body hot or cold. You can pull outside energy into your body and expel stagnant energy from your body. You are able to choose at will the quantity, quality, and direction of flow of energy in your body. Once you learn how to concentrate your mind and direct LifeParticles, you can change circumstances outside of your body as well.

Water Up, Fire Down

Within your body, energy flows in a specific circuit called Su Seung Hwa Gang, or "Water Up, Fire Down" (water rises, fire sinks). The energy in your body is divided into two general categories that are based on temperature. The warm energy of fire is mostly generated in the deep organs, especially the brain, heart, and liver; the cool energy of water is produced in the kidneys.

When you are healthy, warm fire energy from the head and heart flows down the energy pathway in the center of the front of your body to your lower abdomen, which makes your abdomen warm. The fire energy in the abdomen activates the water energy in the kidneys as fire boils and vaporizes water, causing it to rise up the energy pathway in the center of your back to your head. Then, the water energy that has risen up to your head pushes down any fire energy in the head and heart to the lower abdomen. And the circuit continues.

This ideal energy circuit keeps your head cool and a fire in your belly, which is optimal for your overall health. With a cool head, your mind is calm and peaceful and your concentration, judgment, and creativity are enhanced. With a warm abdomen, your digestive, reproductive, and endocrine functions operate normally.

In contrast to this healthy state, when Water Up, Fire Down energy flow is reversed, you will become "hotheaded" and experience headaches, racing thoughts, lack of concentration, and insomnia. The inside of your mouth may become

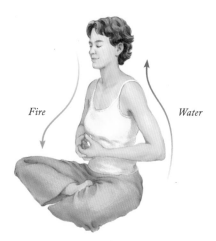

Fire   *Water*

Water Up, Fire Down energy circulation

dry and taste bitter, and your heartbeat may become irregular. In this condition, not only will you be tired and anxious, but you will also feel discomfort and your shoulders and neck may become stiff. Additionally, if warm energy does not sink to your abdomen and cold energy gathers there instead, your intestines will become stiff and you'll develop abnormalities in your digestive, reproductive, and endocrine functions in the form of indigestion, constipation, or issues with your menstrual cycle.

Having a reversed energy flow over long periods can develop into more serious complications, such as high blood pressure, heart attack, or stroke. Applying the principle of Water Up, Fire Down to cool your head and warm your abdomen is an easy yet amazing secret for maintaining your health.

Water Up, Fire Down can be witnessed in nature as well. The sun sending down radiant heat is an example of a fire down phenomenon. Receiving that thermal energy, water evaporates to become vapor and rises into the sky. That is a water up phenomenon. All plants receive the fire energy sent down by the sun. The roots of plants suck up water energy from the ground. Plants flower and bear fruit by combining descending fire and rising water. Water Up, Fire Down, then, is a natural circulation of energy that leads to growth and change.

Poor Energy Circulation Causes Problems

Although a perfect energy system is built into our body, most people don't even know that it exists. Even if they do know it, many don't know how to operate it. As a result, as we go about our lives, we do things that disrupt our energy system. Stress, bad habits, negative thinking, and poor posture all block the proper functioning of the system.

Many ailments in modern life are related to stress and the condition of the mind, both of which determine the state of energy in the body. "Good health" is a state in which energy circulates smoothly in your body. Psychological tension influences the body the moment it begins in the mind. This reflects the principle Energy Follows Where the Mind Goes. When you have negative, harmful mental states, like strain, pressure, anxiety, overwhelm, irritability, insecurity, or nervousness, that mind-set generates energy of that character. This stagnant energy blocks the natural flow of energy. This negatively impacts the blood and cells, which eventually manifests as disease in the corresponding organs. The buildup of such stagnant energy, conversely, has an effect on the mind, causing more stress. This may even lead to mental symptoms, such as depression or insomnia. In most of these cases, improving energy circulation improves the symptoms.

Charge Your Energy with LifeParticles

I have witnessed countless examples of natural healing, great and small, in which people just open up their energy pathways and let energy flow through them—and symptoms amazingly vanish as if they had never even been there.

Most energy training, through various physical and mental techniques, involves bringing in fresh, pure LifeParticles to push through blockages of stagnant energy and fill the body's chakras. Chakras are like your body's unseen batteries and are where LifeParticles centrally collect. When a computer or smartphone battery is almost depleted, it sends a blinking signal that tells you to recharge it. Your body's recharge signal is any abnormality or discomfort you may experience that is physical, mental, or emotional.

The lower the charge of your chakras, the greater the obstacles to your overall health. Those who are physically lethargic or easily tired, who have weakened resistance to stress, or who have trouble controlling their emotions, are people with low energy in their chakras. In this low energy state, our resistance to stress is weakened, creating a self-perpetuating cycle.

Your chakras are your energy centers; when your center is weak, you are easily influenced by the energy around you. However, when your chakras are sufficiently charged by life energy, they become a sturdy, pillar-like energy center not easily shaken by external energy. With a strong center, you are able to stabilize and control the energy of your body and mind. Therefore, you become able to effectively operate your body's energy system by charging your chakras with LifeParticles.

After much research, I have created several methods over the years for charging and developing the energy system of the human body as quickly and effectively as possible. LifeParticle Meditation, using the MindScreen, is the most recent and aligned with the current times. In designing them, I tuned into the frequency of spiritual awakening that I believe the earth and human race are now welcoming.

Since we are living in an age of advanced information technology with global information distributed at a shockingly rapid pace, we are feeling how unseen information changes the material world as well as the consciousness of individuals.

When you create a strong center, your body and mind become better able to process the influx of information that is always around you. Moreover, your mind has a better ability to move LifeParticles and manifest what you want. By charging your chakras with LifeParticles and fully activating your energy system, I predict that you will be able to enter a new state of consciousness.

Five Phenomena Caused by LifeParticles

When you charge your chakras and fill your meridians with LifeParticles, you may experience different sensations in your body. Typical among these are vibration, a sense of heat, a feeling of electric current, light, and enhanced consciousness. These sensations happen in the course of the chakras recovering their original, healthy state.

Vibration

We human beings are, like all other life-forms on the earth, vibration-producing creatures. The ceaseless beating of your heart and pounding of your brain waves are examples of vibration; even the endless rotation and revolution of the earth, the countless stars, and the galaxy are examples of vibration. Everything in the cosmos is vibrating energy. It is always moving and changing. Chakras, too, are bundles of vibrating LifeParticles. If the vibration of the LifeParticles in your chakras is vigorous, your chakras are healthy; if their vibration is weak, their condition is poor.

When you fill your body with LifeParticles, the activity of the energy in your whole body, including your chakras, increases. LifeParticles break through blockages in your meridians and energy points, causing them, and subsequently your tissues, to vibrate like a water hose that swings and pulses rapidly when the water is first turned on at full blast. This physical vibration is the first phenomenon caused by LifeParticles. Vibration can take a variety of forms that, depending on a person's physical condition, can range from subtle energy vibrations to intense vibrations that violently shake the body.

Heat

Physical vibration then generates heat that you can feel in a specific area or in your body overall. A sense of heat, the second phenomenon caused by LifeParticles, is evidence that healing is in progress. Once your chakras are healed and charged by LifeParticles, they return to their original, healthy temperature; the lower chakras grow warmer, and the higher chakras grow cooler.

Electric Current

The third phenomenon caused by LifeParticles is a feeling of electric current; this causes the sudden contraction of muscles, and can result in heat and slight or vigorous vibration. Subtle electric currents flow in the human body and are generated by the movement of ions across cell membranes. A steady concentration of these ions is maintained on either side of the cell membranes of nerve and muscle cells until excitation opens ion channels and allows them to pass through, creating a bioelectric current into and down the cell. This is the current picked up by brain wave measurements, electrocardiograms, and electromyograms. You can feel this current yourself when you focus on your body as your chakras are charged during LifeParticle Meditation. The tingling or shock you may experience is accompanied by the joy and happiness that naturally occur when your chakras have been sufficiently charged.

Light

The fourth phenomenon caused by LifeParticles is light. Light is especially seen when LifeParticles heal and charge your sixth and seven chakras. At that time, your MindScreen gradually grows brighter and that light goes out from your head, passes your chest, and spreads to your whole body. Ultimately, your entire body could feel wrapped in light. The light that pours into your head and chest carries feelings of infinite love and indescribable joy and bliss with it. You may even find yourself shedding tears of gratitude as your heart opens to that light of love and life.

Enhanced Consciousness

The fifth effect of LifeParticles is enhancement of consciousness. With your energy system fully charged and flowing well, your mental and emotional blocks are removed and your heart and mind are open to pure LifeParticles. This propels you into a new state of consciousness—one of infinite love, joy, bliss, gratitude, oneness, and deep peace.

Five Stages of LifeParticle Vibration

Vibration is the most distinctive phenomenon of LifeParticle Meditation. It can take a variety of forms, from subtle energy vibrations to intense vibrations that violently shake the body —all of which, as noted previously, manifest according to the state of a person's physical condition. In addition, how vibration expresses itself in your body evolves according to how deeply and how long you have meditated.

First Stage: Conscious Vibration
In the beginning of a meditation session, vibration may occur automatically. If that's the case, all you need to do is let go of your thinking and entrust your body to it without trying to suppress it. You may not feel vibration at all, however. That's okay. Sometimes you may not be focused enough to create or sense energy flow, or you may not have enough energy. In that case, get the vibration started by shaking your body on purpose. Vibrating your body consciously in this way can get your mind quiet enough to go deeper into a meditative mind-set. Conscious vibration is similar to how your body and mind are gradually put at ease and your thinking settles down, such as when you rock back and forth in a rocking chair. I call this conscious vibration the first of five stages of vibration. If you concentrate easily, you can skip the first stage and begin immediately with the second or third stage.

Second Stage: Semiconscious Vibration
As your mind quiets and your awareness goes deeper into your mind from your conscious vibration, you can enter a semiconscious state in which, even though you are aware that you're vibrating, you gradually resonate with the rhythm of the vibration and start to feel your body moving automatically. This is the second stage of vibration. As the vibration clears any energy blocks, your body will start to fill with energy, mak-

ing you feel warm as your thoughts fall silent. LifeParticles are starting to charge your chakras at this stage. Continue to follow the rhythm of the vibration and the vibration will naturally become stronger and deeper.

Third Stage: Unconscious Vibration

The third level of vibration occurs when you enter an unconscious state. In this state, it becomes difficult to stop your vibration. The natural healing abilities of your autonomic nervous system are stimulated as LifeParticles move more vigorously and you become more connected to the automatic, unconscious processes of your body. With a single thought, you can direct this healing ability to where you need it. If you think "shoulder," or if you visualize or feel your shoulder, much more vigorous vibration or movement will occur there. In this way, you can concentrate on the parts of your body you want to heal as you vibrate, and you can also heal your chakras, one by one, starting with your first chakra.

Fourth Stage: Subtle Energy Vibration

After your chakras are healed to a certain degree through this unconscious vibration, your vibrations will gradually subside. If you control your breathing for a while, you will go on to the next stage of vibration. The fourth stage of vibration involves subtle energy vibrations that occur internally and are not readily apparent externally. If you observe the chakras in your body during this stage, you'll be able to feel the vibrations of energy taking place in them. If you do Chakra Breathing, which is explained in a later chapter of this book, and you concentrate on each of them, one by one, beginning with your first chakra, your chakras will be charged with LifeParticles.

In the course of gradually descending to the very bottom of your unconscious mind through Chakra Breathing, old emotions or images of old memories connected with each of your chakras may come up on your MindScreen. Some of them are dark, heavy energy stuck deep inside your chakras that have been suppressing the normal activities of the chakras. This energy has built up over time, and may even have reached the point where it developed into diseases of body and mind. If you fully realize that these emotions or memories actually caused the problems in your body and mind, and allow them to leave your body, they will do so.

Clearing your heart chakra of these old emotions and memories is especially important. Breathe as you concentrate on your heart chakra to make your chest feel more comfortable. You may even find yourself weeping as your emotions are cleared and brightened. When you can breathe deeply and naturally from your chest, then the energy in your heart has been purified and healed.

Once the energy of your heart chakra is purified in this way, pure energy will rise from it and pass through your fifth chakra into your sixth chakra. That energy will fill your brain and heal every part of it. As you watch the process with your MindScreen, you may notice parts of your brain that once felt hard, dark, and stiff gradually becoming brighter and more flexible.

Fifth Stage: Vibration of Light

When the brain is full of bright, healthy energy, the fifth stage of vibration occurs. Rather than a physical vibration, it is a vibration of light—your consciousness vibrates at the level of light. A bright light shines in front of your forehead and eyes, and then pierces deeply into your brain. When that light descends into your chest and illuminates your whole body, you will feel deep gratitude for the light of life and infinite love, as well as an indescribable joy and gladness. In this state, the boundaries between you and the rest of the world dissolve, and you may be able to perceive both the empty space of the universe and the potential energy that composes it. You are no longer able to notice that you are meditating because you are fully immersed in the experience. This is true meditation and is an energetic representation of the zero point. Such a state of unconsciousness is the most effective for projecting what you want on your MindScreen. Genuine creation becomes possible at this stage.

To experience this fifth stage, you must achieve a state of nothingness, a state of pure consciousness in which your thinking has ceased and your emotions have been purified. For this, it's important that you do Chakra Vibration and Breathing repeatedly to purify your body and mind and fill them with LifeParticles. Once each of your chakras is completely charged by LifeParticles, you will be able to experience the fifth stage of vibration, the vibration of light.

• • •

The energy of life entering and leaving your body
flows evenly throughout the universe.
With that current, the mind of the cosmos
communicates with all things.

• • •

chapter 6

Meet the LifeParticle Sun

When your sixth chakra becomes more active and the vibrations of life energy become vigorous, you may experience a light pouring into your head. What is that light? How do you see it with your eyes closed, even in a dark place?

Some traditions say that the light originates in the pineal gland, which is a pinecone-shaped endocrine gland in the diencephalon of the brain. Most sections of the brain form laterally symmetrical pairs in the right and left hemispheres, but the pineal gland exists as a single element in the deepest part of the brain. This gland detects light that enters the head through the scalp and secretes a neurotransmitter called melatonin, which coordinates sleep and reproductive cycles and regulates biorhythms. René Descartes, a French philosopher who spent a great deal of time researching the pineal gland, called it the "principal seat of the soul," and placed such significance on it that he believed it to be the point of connection between the body and the intellect.

The pineal gland appears early in fetal development, when it is reddish-gray and the shape of an oval grain of rice approximately five to eight millimeters in size. Under a microscope, the pineal gland is seen to consist of a myriad of particles that look like tiny grains of sand. In living tissue, these grains vibrate at a high speed. In dead organisms, particle movement has stopped, and the particles stick to one another. The pineal gland is very well developed in lower animals, and is composed of an eye-like structure. In higher-level animals, however, it appears to be an "atrophied eye" with reduced function.

The pineal gland is largest in humans in early childhood, and begins to atrophy and calcify after about the age of ten. Calcification rates vary widely by country and tend to increase with age, according to Robert Zimmerman's research, with calcification occurring in an estimated 40 percent of Americans by their seventeenth year. As the gland calcifies, the space between the particles gradually shrinks and their vibration slows.

Many traditions symbolically express the light seen in a deep meditative state. The Third Eye spoken of by Hinduism and Taoism in the East, the Eye of Horus of ancient Egypt, the pinecone statue in the Vatican, and the pinecone carved on the staff that the pope uses are all examples of this. Buddhist scriptures also describe a light shining from the forehead of the Buddha that illuminates the world.

These various traditions seem to describe the same thing in the end—that is, those phenomena that occur when the energy of the sixth and seventh chakra are activated. LifeParticle Meditation is an easy and fast method through which you can experience these wonders. In deep LifeParticle Meditation, when your consciousness and energy state become extremely pure and sensitive, and the particles vibrate with high frequency, the pineal gland in the sixth chakra seems to detect the vibration as a form of light. Your third eye, your MindScreen, goes into operation in this way, and you come to experience an ecstasy of light.

In this state, you may feel something like oil or a sticky liquid being secreted in your brain and descending along your spinal cord. It feels as if oil poured from the crown of your head into your brain is flowing down to your chest, abdomen, and whole body through your endocrine and nervous systems. Through this experience, your brain and body, which once felt dry and solid, now seem fluid, moist, and flexible, giving you the feeling that you've recovered the energy of youth.

Throughout the ages, countless people have been trying to find medicines that bring youth and long life, as well as special substances that bring enlightenment and blessings. Examples of these are the Philosopher's Stone; the Elixir of Life; the Nectar of the Gods; and the Fountain of Youth, which are found in the ancient traditions of both East and West. Similar to these are the manna; the Holy Spirit and holy anointing oil of the Bible; the ambrosia that was the food and drink of the gods in Greek mythology; and the ojas of

Hinduism, which means "fluid of life." All of these can be related to the phenomenon that occurs in your body while you are in a deep meditative state of consciousness with high energy. Rather than elixirs that need to be ingested, why not feel the true Elixir of Life secreted in your own brain by the illumination of the light of life?

The Moment of Meeting the LifeParticle Sun

This light you experience in deep meditation is what I've named the "LifeParticle Sun." This light is seen when your idle thoughts and emotions have quieted, when your brain is healed by and charged full of life energy, and when your consciousness has become truly pure. It is not something you have intentionally imagined, or something someone else has artificially created and is sending to you. It is just a natural phenomenon, a phenomenon of life that has always been shining there "from the beginning." This light was there before you were born and even before the earth existed; and it will continue to exist even after you have left this world, even after the earth is no more.

The LifeParticle Sun is shining on all of us in the fundamental level of reality, just as the sun illuminates the earth in the tangible physical world. It is light arising out of the source of life energy.

This light is a universal phenomenon anyone can experience once the body's energy system has been restored to its original, healthy state and your consciousness has been brightened. It is always shining, but it is usually invisible to the five senses. It can be seen when you enter a state of pure consciousness and your mind's eye, your third eye, opens.

Jane Owens described her encounter with the LifeParticle Sun in this way.

"For a twenty-one day period, I was doing LifeParticle Meditation at a set time every morning. It was the most precious time of my day. First, through preparatory training, I got the energy circulating well in my body, and ensured that warm energy was accumulating—especially in my lower abdomen. After that, I did meditation with breathing for a while. At some point, I could feel warm energy rising from my first and second chakras along my spine. When the energy circulated in and healed my brain, my sixth chakra, a clear indigo-blue light would appear before my eyes. When I continued to concentrate, the light sometimes spun in a clockwise direction, gradually spreading out and expanding. If I kept my heart wide open and accepted that light with my whole heart, the light illuminated my entire brain and brought a smile to my face before I even realized it.

"One day, as the light poured down into my chest, it seemed to be healing the emotions that were in my heart. As the beautiful blue light continued to push like waves into my heart, into my whole body, I felt it caressing and healing my heart and all my cells. Then a thought suddenly crossed my mind: Where does this light come from? Immediately following that, a voice rose out of my heart: 'The light is coming from

the source of life. I'm now being connected with the source of life.' Through the beam of light pouring into my chest, I could feel with my whole heart that I was connected as one with the source where that light began.

"The light seemed to be saying this to me: 'I love you. I love you. I love you.' My heart was deeply moved by that message of love, which I heard from the source of life, and hot tears started flowing from my eyes. It was a feeling of great, complete love you cannot get anywhere, or from anyone, in the world; it was a feeling of complete unity. 'Thank you. Thank you. Thank you for loving me.' Gratitude flowed endlessly from my heart along with those tears. The feeling of the light of life that had flowed out of the source of life pouring into my heart, into my whole body, was the greatest experience I've ever had since being born into this world. The light of the LifeParticle Sun was itself complete love, a complete blessing."

Many other people share a similar experience with Jane in regard to the LifeParticle Sun. Once you are connected as one with the LifeParticle Sun in this way, you will be filled with infinite gladness and gratitude, and you will get a feeling of complete unity, relief, and peace, as if you had returned to your soul's home.

The LifeParticle Sun is the mind of the cosmos, the light of the universe's divinity coming from the source of life. Cosmic Mind is infinite love itself. Anyone can experience the light of infinite love coming from the LifeParticle Sun if their energy system is restored to its original, healthy state, and they enter a state of pure consciousness. You can truly live your life holding the LifeParticle Sun in your heart and illuminate those around you with the warmth and brightness of the LifeParticle Sun.

Macrocosmic Energy Circulation

Just as LifeParticles need to circulate freely within our body's energy system, for true health, happiness, peace, or enlightenment, they also need to circulate between our self and the life energy of the cosmos. There are two levels for circulating energy through the body's energy system. The first is microcosmic circulation; the second is macrocosmic circulation.

Your body is like a little universe. The Water Up, Fire Down energy circuit is microcosmic circulation within the universe of your body. While it is important for this circuit to flow unimpeded, you cannot achieve a perfect state of health through this alone. No matter how much you try to resolve an issue by improving your microcosmic circulation, you will just be like a gerbil running on its wheel. You cannot circulate great energy by this inner rotation alone. You must add macrocosmic circulation and circulate energy with the universe at large. Macrocosmic circulation invigorates the circulation of energy between your body and the universe. Just as rice crops on dry land will grow well when you irrigate them with water drawn from a big lake or river, the vital energy of our bodies and minds will become invigorated only if we solidly connect to the universe and its vast sea of life energy.

The energy system in your body is not independent and it does not operate in isolation; it is intimately connected with the life energy of the universe. The invisible life energy of the universe is ceaselessly being supplied to you through your breathing and your meridian points. When you truly realize that your life force is not maintained by your own independent power, but by the greater energy at large, your small, finite self gains the power to draw in that energy.

LifeParticle Meditation is a method to help you strengthen your connection with the LifeParticles of the universe. Through visualization in this method, the LifeParticle Sun provides you with a never-ending supply of LifeParticles. For example, you can imagine it shining brightly in front of your forehead, where the opening to your sixth chakra lies, or above the energy point to your seventh chakra at the top of your head.

The crown of the head at the highest part of the body is one of the best gates for receiving cosmic energy. If you focus your attention there, you can experience LifeParticles entering your body as if they were falling on your head like dew, like a flow of water, or like poured oil. All you have to do is think of your body as a vessel and continue accepting LifeParticles, storing them in your head, chest, and lower abdomen, and circulating them throughout your chakras and your whole body.

Let the LifeParticle Sun always shine for you. Don't let it disappear. Charge yourself with bright LifeParticles from the LifeParticle Sun to maintain a macrocosmic circuit with the life energy of the universe and live in a pure, bright capsule of LifeParticles surrounding your body.

Becoming One with the LifeParticle Sun

How strongly or easily the LifeParticle Sun comes to you in meditation depends upon the purity of your mind and the level of your concentration and energy circulation. Stages of evolution of consciousness are commonly compared to the different levels of brightness. A person's consciousness can be said to be "bright" or "dark." When you're feeling bad or your energy is down, your consciousness is darker. When you meditate in that state, it will take time and difficulty to experience bright light. Conversely, when you're feeling good and your body's energy is circulating well, your consciousness is brighter. In that state, it's not a big leap to experience bright light in meditation—in fact, it can happen rather quickly. The condition of your body and mind reflects the state of your consciousness in that moment, and the brightness of the light you experience in a meditative state will vary in accordance with your state of consciousness.

You'll see the light of the LifeParticle Sun when your mind's eye, not your physical eyes, has opened. Opening your mind's eye means the development of a kind of sixth sense. When your consciousness is closed and dark, you only believe in the world that you see and hear within your own knowledge, and you close your mind to everything else, such as the invisible world of energy. When your mind's eye opens and your consciousness becomes bright, however, you become able to discern both the visible material world and the invisible spiritual world. It is similar to when a room is dark and your visibility is impaired; you can't really recognize objects in that room. However, when you turn on a bright light, you can clearly see everything, even things that are tiny or far away. Thus, when your consciousness is dark, your mind is limited and you can only believe what you see immediately before your eyes; and when your consciousness is brighter, your mind broadens because your mind's eye, which is capable of seeing into the unseen world, opens up.

In the brightness of the LifeParticle Sun in your mind's eye, you automatically see the principles of the world and realize the essence of life: "My essence is LifeParticles that have come from the source of life. My physical self is born and dies, but at the level of LifeParticles, I have never been born, and I do not die. Birth is an event created by the coming together of LifeParticles, and death is merely a scattering of LifeParticles. At the level of LifeParticles, I am an eternal being, unborn and undying."

Similar to the elementary particles that vibrate even in a zero-point field, the LifeParticles that compose your consciousness, which is the substance of who you are, are not destroyed. They merely gather and scatter as they travel back and forth between the visible and the invisible. Those who have realized that they are LifeParticles know the true meaning of eternal life. We are eternal beings, lumps of LifeParticles that begin in the source of life, and we live on a ceaseless supply of LifeParticles until we return to the source of life.

The process of brightening your consciousness and becoming one with the LifeParticle Sun is for recovering the zero point. The zero point is a state of pure consciousness free from the obsession, discrimination, and emotion that originate in the ego. When we strip these away, we reach our true nature, our original state that existed before we accumulated thoughts, preconceptions, judgments, and experiences over the course of our lives. This accumulation you have labeled as "you" does not exist in a state of zero. It is merely an image you have painted in order to interact with the world. In the same way, there is no "other" either. The concept of "other" exists to define "you." In the place of "you" and "other" is a sense of being that encompasses everything. This being that you really are lies beyond your ego because it cannot be contained or defined. It was never born, and it never dies. It simply exists, and it is everything.

The zero point is a place you can go to free yourself from the tumult of emotions and the uncertainty of living. It's a place of peace, unity, and knowingness. Rather than being empty, which you may associate with zero or nothingness, there is total fullness and completion because it is a place without boundaries or definition, and one in which everything can exist simultaneously. It is a place of complete and unlimited potential from which you can manifest anything. Therefore, you can only access it completely when you've stripped away all of the thought patterns and forms you've already created.

LifeParticle Meditation enables you to clear your thoughts and emotions and align the frequency of your consciousness to that of the LifeParticle Sun; it brings you to the zero point. Once you recover the zero point, you may find that you respect yourself at a deeper level. Because you awaken to the essence of your life by obtaining a zero consciousness that is purified of everything, you may realize that you are a noble living being, regardless of the situations or environments confronting you or the assessments of those around you. In gratitude for life and its blessings, these words may well up within you: "Thank you for granting me life even for this one day today. I will make good use of this precious life energy."

When you have such a great awakening concerning the essence of your life, you will be able to see yourself, and everything else, through an integrated consciousness at the essential level of LifeParticles. Respect and love for life will flow automatically from your heart, and you will be able to share with others the bright, clear, blessed energy you have received from the LifeParticle Sun.

Once you know how to become one with the LifeParticle Sun, you will not need to seek love and blessings from others; you can receive them for yourself. As you enter the state of zero-point consciousness and become one with the LifeParticle Sun, you can be fully charged with LifeParticles, the shining grains of love and blessing.

And, if you want, you can always share the blessings of those LifeParticles with others. The moment you do, you become someone who sends blessings to yourself instead of waiting for blessings to come from elsewhere. To share the blessings of LifeParticles, you have to imagine yourself always connected with the LifeParticle Sun. Thus, sharing blessings with others is a shortcut for receiving blessings yourself.

I believe that a world overflowing with love, a harmonious, peaceful world, will automatically develop if an increasing number of people experience such realization and enlightenment firsthand. The beginning of all these things is acknowledging and experiencing ourselves as what we really are: "I am bright LifeParticles."

Encountering the light of the LifeParticle Sun and the truth behind it is a natural phenomenon that occurs for anyone when they develop their energy system and practice using it. If you have truly and deeply experienced the brightness and warmth of the LifeParticle Sun, you can shine light on those around you with its brightness and warmth. You can shine as another little LifeParticle Sun!

Experiencing brightness in meditation is not a one-time experience; it is something you continue to develop throughout your life. You can take it deeper and deeper, until the most profound truth is part of your everyday outlook. Going a step further, you can then manifest that truth in your daily life. That's why I always say, "Enlightenment that isn't shared is not true enlightenment." If your experience ends as no more than an experience, without actually changing your life, then it is merely an illusion. It's little different from watching the fantasy world of bright lights in a movie theater, and then leaving. If a new consciousness has awakened in your brain through your experiences, then you must implant that consciousness throughout your body, in each and every one of your cells. Your thoughts, words, actions, and lifestyle will change as you do this.

When you meditate, you are in a state of maximum energy. When you go back to your daily life, however, you return to your previous state of inertial energy, to your habits of life, because your training isn't connected with how you live. Thus, your practice ends up being something separate from how you lead your life. Although it won't be easy at first, you can reduce the gap that develops between your meditation practice and your lifestyle by continuing to do LifeParticle Meditation and consciously visualizing the LifeParticle Sun as often as possible. Over time, you'll get a taste of the joys of meditation becoming your life, and your life becoming meditation.

Receive the bright light from the LifeParticle Sun through LifeParticle Meditation and your energy will become brighter. Keep growing that bright energy and let it fill your heart and your life fully. Then spread that bright light to the world. Like the sun, the bright energy from your heart will spread out to the ends of the earth.

chapter 7

Charge Yourself Up 24/7

It is no exaggeration to say that we ultimately live our lives to be joyful and happy. We wouldn't want to go on living if our lives were bereft of joy. We ceaselessly thirst for something that could bring greater vitality and meanings to our lives, and we want to be happier and more joyful.

What, then, is genuine happiness? Do you feel happy? If you feel happy, then why do you feel happy? If you're unhappy, then what do you think makes you unhappy?

I once saw a TV documentary on happiness. A reporter asked people passing by on the street, "What would make you happier?" Most people—male, female, young and old—answered that they would be happier if they had money, a car, a house, or some other material possession. Does having a lot of money really make you happy?

Of course, to feel a sense of happiness, you need a basic environment in which a stable life is possible. Is a person happier the more money he has, though? How much is our sense of happiness determined by material plenty?

University of Illinois at Urbana-Champaign psychologist Dr. Ed Diener and colleagues compared the happiness of forty-nine of America's 400 richest people selected by *Forbes* magazine to a random sample of U.S. citizens living in the same areas. In the happiness indexes measured, the rich scored only slightly but significantly higher. Thirty-seven percent of them had a lower score on one happiness scale than the average of the group of typical citizens. This shatters our preconception that the wealthiest people must be truly happy, since they have so much and can enjoy whatever they want. Diener found that wealth played only a small part in the happiness of the wealthiest Americans. Further, the wealthy people surveyed gave these reasons for what they thought makes people happy: first, love, friends, and family; second, self-actualization; third, self-esteem; and fourth, good health. The less affluent people gave similar reasons for their happiness, although they were more concerned about their health. Both groups strongly felt that money can be helpful to happiness if used correctly, but that it is no guarantee of happiness.

In a later experiment, Diener analyzed data from a Gallup World Poll and discovered that income was a moderately strong indicator of how a person evaluated their life but a much weaker indicator of positive and negative feelings. This result is supported by an examination of a 2008 to 2009 Gallup Poll on 450,000 Americans by Princeton University researchers Daniel Kahneman and Angus Deaton. They found with every doubling of income people tended to say they were more satisfied with their lives. However, money mattered only up to about $75,000 in whether people said they experienced a lot of enjoyment, laughter, smiling, anger, stress, or worry. After that, money didn't buy more happiness.

A study in South Korea similarly showed that once incomes climbed above $4,000 per month, little difference was seen in levels of happiness, even as that amount increased. In other words, levels of happiness were comparable for people earning $4,000 a month and people earning $6,000 a month. Happiness did not increase with every thousand dollars in additional income; rather, once a certain level of income had been exceeded, no matter how much the amount increased, happiness did not increase that much with it.

What Does Make Us Happy?

I read this news article on the Internet. One Austrian millionaire realized that he had become unhappy because of his wealth and donated all his assets of 3 million pounds (4.8 million U.S. dollars). He gave up his fashionable villa with a view of the Alps, his farm in France, and sold his glider, his expensive car, and his business. Feeling freedom as he liquidated his assets, he said, "I'm thinking of not leaving behind anything at all. Money has the opposite effect. It keeps happiness from coming." He planned to move from his villa in the Alps to a little cottage or rented room. Born in a poor home, he said, "I have long believed that more wealth and luxury meant more happiness but, as time has passed, I've come to think, 'I should stop my extravagance and consumption, and begin really living.'" He added, "I got the feeling that I was working like a slave for things I didn't want or need. I realized how horrible a five-star life is without soul and without feeling."

His last words really touched me. Happiness does not come through certain conditions. It's not like you can become eternally happy because you have obtained something you want. According to research, your happiness increases when you get something you want; however, once a certain amount of time passes, that feeling of happiness falls to a level similar to what it was before.

Happiness does not come only when you get something even greater. It's something you feel when you hope for less and are sufficiently satisfied with what you have now. That's why you can't help but look back over your life at least once after you've seen someone who, despite losing both arms, expresses life happily, dancing and writing and drawing with the two feet they have.

Genuine happiness does not come from external environment or conditions, nor is it like an object or event that someone else brings to you. Most of those who feel an ongoing sense of happiness in their lives, and not just in some moment or a single event, say that happiness is a small, plain sense of satisfaction spread throughout their daily lives. People say they're happy when they feel inner satisfaction with themselves and their present lives, regardless of whether they have much or little, whether they are in lofty or lowly positions, or whether they find themselves in good conditions or bad. In other words, they are grateful to be alive and for the very lives given them, and tend to create their own happiness instead of waiting for happiness to come to them.

The Source of Energy Never Runs Out

The energy of joy is a source that allows us to live our lives more happily. Without joy, a person's life would be boring to the point of being cracked and dry like a desert. To obtain the energy of joy in whatever form, people look for someone to love and a goal into which they can pour their energy. They say that life is worth living when they can feel the joy of achieving something, whether it's money, prestige, or power. That's why, desperate for love and success, everyone suffers from stress as they engage in selfish competition. Yet even those who have seized love and success ultimately feel a fundamental sense of emptiness and loneliness that nothing can fill.

It seems to me that what modern people fear most is "boredom." Being bored means that you don't find meaning or excitement in what you are doing and your energy of joy has been depleted. In order to charge themselves with the energy of joy and excitement, people ceaselessly meet with others, a friend or lover, perhaps; seek delicious food; sightsee; or sit in front of a TV or computer screen. If this is not enough to relieve the boredom of life off-line, many of us escape our real world to enjoy our alter ego life online. The entertainment industry is growing daily due to the demands of modern people who fear boredom and continually want fresh stimulation.

There are many sources for joy in our lives, but you should know the one that you already have is the most powerful. The greatest form of entertainment is having fun with your self.

It is about discovering the world of infinite life energy within you and making use of it. When your consciousness enters the world of pure life energy, you will feel the energy of joy and love and happiness coming from the light of the LifeParticle Sun—a light that cannot be compared with anything in the world.

That light is like an oasis that never runs dry, one that can fundamentally quench your long thirst. Once you taste such fundamental love and joy from the LifeParticle Sun, you no longer need to search for joy in other people or other things. To recharge your joy, all you have to do is plug directly into the source of life energy. That energy is unlimited and never runs out because it is the energy of unconditional love that doesn't discriminate among people.

This joy grows even greater when you share it with the people around you. The joy you feel when you become a small LifeParticle Sun and share its brightness and warmth with those around you is indescribably great. It is the joy of a pure soul who doesn't seek reward, a joy obtained from benefiting others and making them happy.

What Does Happiness Look Like?

How happy are you right now? If you're happy, then what sort of feeling is it? There is a happiness index that different surveys generally use as a method for determining a person's degree of happiness. However, I propose another method for very easily measuring how happy you are right now. All you need to do is concentrate your awareness on your body and check the physical sensations you have right now. Sensations in the body are feelings of energy, and energy is influenced by the mind. So the energy of happiness is bound to manifest physically in people who feel happy.

When they are feeling good, Koreans say, "Kibun johta," which literally means, "the distribution of energy is harmonious." This indicates that energy is circulating well in your body and your chakras are sufficiently charged with LifeParticles. When you are happy, your energy system is working properly—that is, your lower abdomen is warm, your chest feels comfortable and open, your head is clear and cool, your face looks cheerful and bright, and a gentle smile can't resist appearing on your face. On the other hand, a frowning face means there is poor energy circulation in your chest and brain.

Try putting a smile on your face right now. If you observe the condition of your body while you smile, you'll feel your respiration growing more comfortable, which sends more oxygen to your brain. Quietly try to feel the inside of your brain as you continue to smile. As time goes by, those with a well-developed ability to sense energy may get a fluid feeling, as if a liquid is flowing in their brains. Sweet saliva will also flow in your mouth. Feeling more fluid and having more saliva in your mouth is evidence that your energy is circulating well—simply from smiling. Just as a smile naturally appears when you are happy and your energy system is full and circulating without obstruction, making a smile when you're feeling a little down or low on energy can give your energy system a boost of LifeParticles. That smile will be hard to identify, such as the smile on a statue of the Buddha or the smile of Mona Lisa as painted by Leonardo da Vinci. This is the most ideal energy state.

This ideal energy state is one in which LifeParticles are working at peak performance. Through LifeParticles, you can get help for continuing such a positive state or for maintaining it as long as possible.

Positive LifeParticles and Negative LifeParticles

LifeParticles are originally in a neutral, indeterminate state of limitless possibilities. What determines the quality of positivity or negativity is the kind of information given to the LifeParticles. Think of it as pure white light that changes its color when it is filtered through colored lenses. When information is added, LifeParticles move and change according to that information. If bright, positive information is added to LifeParticles, they become bright and positive. However, if dark, negative information is added to them, they act as dark, negative energy. What changes the characteristics of neutral LifeParticles, then, is the mind.

What you experience through LifeParticle Meditation is pure LifeParticles. When your thoughts and emotions become quiet and purified and you reach the zero point, your consciousness cannot help become lighter and purer. Then you become able to experience brilliant brightness and unconditional love. Accessing this light and love in the world of pure life energy and consciousness is impossible when you have negative thoughts or emotions.

If your consciousness is negative, it means that you have not yet reached the zero point, where pure consciousness and limitless possibilities exist. Instead, you remain stuck in your Thinking Brain and Emotional Brain, both of which function within the constraints of separation and limitation. Instead of recognizing that you are one with everything, your Thinking Brain insists that you are separate from everything.

All thoughts of separation, and the accompanying emotions caused by these thoughts, change the properties of LifeParticles. For example, if you are angry or if you resent someone, those thoughts and emotions color LifeParticles in a negative way, which not only have a negative impact on your body, but also influence the other person as well.

In your everyday life, you will have experienced your consciousness becoming negative or your mood becoming foul when your energy dropped for no apparent reason. This is a signal that the energy of your chakras is depleted by the negativity of your mind, and you should charge your chakras with LifeParticles. You will recover a "positive state" when you charge your chakras with LifeParticles.

Maintaining a Positive Energy State

Just by quieting your mind and concentrating on how your body feels, you can detect easily whether you are in a positive energy state or not. A typical method is by checking the feeling within your brain. A positive state is a "pleasant brain state." If you get the feeling that your brain is somehow heavy and unclear, it is a signal that a negative energy state in your body has increased. When this happens, just supply every nook and cranny of your brain with fresh oxygen and bright LifeParticles by doing LifeParticle Meditation.

You can even try it right now. Close your eyes and smile gently. Repeat the word "LifeParticles" to yourself and imagine that bright LifeParticles from above your head are pouring down into your whole body. If you do this for even one minute, you'll be able to feel your brain becoming happy as the smile on your lips spreads to the rest of your face and even to your brain. Doing this can help you always maintain the most pleasant mind state.

A positive state is also a state in which your consciousness is open. Being open means that you are ready to respond positively and accept the things that happen in and around you. There's a simple method for determining whether your state is positive and open—just check to see how you generally respond when people around you exhibit certain behaviors or make certain suggestions.

For one type of person, a negative reaction pops out first, habitually and unconsciously, before they even think about it. This person habitually and automatically reacts that way because negative responses have been formed in their brain, causing them to react negatively to almost everything.

A second type reacts positively when other people's actions or proposals are to their liking, and reacts negatively when they are not. Such a person judges immediately whether they like or dislike what others are doing or saying, based on the standards of their own fixed ideas or emotions.

A third type responds first with a positive, open consciousness, without leaping to judgment, and seeks first to discover potential in others' actions or suggestions.

A "positive, open consciousness" means looking at something as it is, without coating it in your own ideas or emotions and, furthermore, looking for hope and potential in it. Thus, when your consciousness is open, you can communicate easily with another person and accept positively that person's actions or suggestions. An open person fundamentally has a respect for all life. Additionally, that person readily accesses cosmic information, because the door of their consciousness is open and they are able to receive needed ideas and inspiration easily. This leads to new creation.

A positive state is also a state of restored naturalness. Naturalness, in this case, means not forcing yourself to create what's not there. You are not making a positive state by artificially pretending to be cheerful and positive. Rather, a positive state is one in which a brightness and cheerfulness flows naturally from within. It is the brightness and warmth of the inner LifeParticle Sun radiating from within you. Since a person's original mind is bright like the sun, all we really have to do is simply restore our mind to the original and most natural state.

LifeParticle Meditation helps you to experience such a positive energy state, that is, a state of open consciousness and a state of restored naturalness, and helps you to maintain that state in your daily life. It is a method for bringing up the bright LifeParticle Sun on your MindScreen to fully charge yourself with LifeParticles.

Connecting to the Source of Happiness

Here is the story of Linda Gorman, who is working all day long, and even while she sleeps, to maintain a state charged with bright LifeParticles. Linda's story illustrates just how deeply our happiness is related to our energy state and how we can utilize LifeParticles to keep a positive energy state for as long as possible.

"I sit down and do LifeParticle Meditation as soon as I get up in the morning," Linda says. "I bring up my MindScreen and accept the bright light of the LifeParticle Sun, which I use to charge my whole body with LifeParticles. I feel the bright, warm light of the LifeParticle Sun shining within me, and I can continually maintain myself in good condition on days I start by charging myself using the LifeParticle Sun like that. Also, I try to have that mind-set in dealing with others.

"I do a lot of computer work in an office. Before I did LifeParticle Meditation, when I worked, I would focus only on the work without realizing what state my body was in, what state my mind was in. Having done that for a while, by the time afternoon rolled around, my head and the back of my neck would grow hotter, my concentration would drop off, and fatigue would rush over me. As the energy in my body would decline, unconsciously my mood would get worse and my attitude would become negative. My power to control stress would also drop off, so I would be easily stressed even by the little irritations around me.

"Lately, though, I think I've learned the secret for always maintaining my body and mind in a positive state. Not only am I diligently doing LifeParticle training every day at home, but I'm receiving LifeParticles at work, too. I imagine that LifeParticles are continuously entering my body, even while I'm doing computer work. Then I feel my mood improve, and a smile comes to my face.

"If I feel like my concentration has weakened or my energy has declined a little bit, I immediately straighten my spine and imagine LifeParticles pouring down into my head and body from above my head. I can feel myself starting to smile as I'm charged with LifeParticles in no time. Thanks to LifeParticles, I can always maintain a bright, positive state, and my brain especially becomes clearer and cooler, so I have fewer distracting thoughts and really concentrate well on my work."

I think happiness is determined by how much time we spend feeling good during the day. About how many hours of your day do you think you are in a positive, happy state?

Happiness is something we create ourselves. To our eyes, the sun appears to rise in the east every day to create a brilliant morning for the earth. The sun, however, does not create the morning alone; the earth also creates it actively as it rotates every day. We shouldn't just wait for happiness, either. Happiness doesn't come when we wait for it; we make it ourselves.

It's empowering to realize that, regardless of our circumstances, we have the power to choose and create our own happiness. Don't seek happiness with conditions. Happiness can only be felt if you don't set any condition, and that's exactly what you feel through LifeParticle Meditation. At the moment you are connected to LifeParticles, you are happy for no reason.

Charging your body and mind with LifeParticles is the secret for creating spontaneous and long-lasting happiness. Remember that the source of happiness never dries out. It's always there, right there. All we need to do to access it is connect to the source.

• • •

We have an innate sensibility for being content,
feeling joyful, and living in happiness without conditions.
Happiness is a natural condition of existence.

• • •

Transmit LifeParticles of Love

So far, I've described LifeParticles as the energy of pureness, brightness, love, bliss, peace, enlightenment, and unity. If I were asked which of these expresses the essence of LifeParticles, however, I would say it was "love." There are many different types and levels of love. LifeParticles are the complete, unconditional love that arises out of a pure soul.

The pure love of LifeParticles can be sent and received once you've integrated several realizations and principles regarding LifeParticles.

The first is the realization that everything, including you, is LifeParticles. Once you realize that you are LifeParticles, other people are LifeParticles, and everything in the universe is all LifeParticles, you will gain the awareness that, ultimately, we are all one.

The second is recovering a sense of connection. Once you know that all are one, it is easy to make the leap to the understanding that all visible things, though they may outwardly appear to be separate from one another, are intimately related to you through LifeParticles. Knowing this truth, you can feel connected to everything around you. When you deal with another person and perceive that person as an aggregate of LifeParticles connected with your own energy, rather than as a separate individual, you will feel compelled to send them kind, positive energy.

The third is always allowing gratitude to remain in your heart. Gratitude is like a fountainhead from which the energy of pure love is always erupting. When you feel genuine gratitude, you feel it in your heart, not in your head. The energy that automatically overflows from you, when gratitude fills your heart, is love. That is why it's important to keep the spring of gratitude in your heart from drying up, and to enable the waters of that spring to grow even more powerful and overflow.

To keep the spring of gratitude in your heart flowing, you have to activate the energy of your heart chakra. Your dissatisfaction and complaints grow and you become passive and negative when the energy in your heart is dark, cold, and weak. When your heart's energy is activated, you are positive and proactive in everything, and share bright, warm energy with others. To activate the pure energy of your heart chakra effectively, fill it with LifeParticles. When bright, warm LifeParticles of love from the LifeParticle Sun fill your heart and body, your body and mind will burst with gratitude.

Instead of keeping LifeParticles for yourself when you are full of gratitude and love, you can't help but send the pure love of LifeParticles to others. That's the nature of love. Think of yourself as a transparent crystal. As you receive the LifeParticles that flow out of the LifeParticle Sun, let them flow untainted through you to other people. In this way, you act as a "LifeParticle Transmitter."

You can give and receive LifeParticles alone or as a group. The method many people use together is called "collaborative healing." It is so powerful that many are experiencing miracles of healing with its practice. The method involves people sitting in a circle and sending LifeParticles to a person sitting in the center who wants healing. If the people sending LifeParticles are not in proximity, they can set a time to do so together and send LifeParticles simultaneously, from wherever they are, to the person in need of healing.

Regardless of what method is used, before sending LifeParticles, everyone should turn on their MindScreen through LifeParticle Meditation. The MindScreen acts as both a control pad and a channel for moving LifeParticles. After opening your MindScreen, you can send LifeParticles to your own body and you can send LifeParticles to other people. What is most important is to have a truly sincere and earnest heart of pure love.

Recovering a sense of oneness as LifeParicles and feeling gratitude and love opens your heart. And when that heart energy activates the unconscious Life Brain in the deep inside of your brain, miracles of healing and transformation happen.

Particles Move through Time and Space

LifeParticles can be sent to anyone, anywhere, and be effective. Brian Wright, who lives in Northern California and learned how to use LifeParticles at a LifeParticle Workshop, discovered this for himself when he and his wife Leanna sent LifeParticles to his wife's mother in Russia. His mother-in-law had had a stroke that left her paralyzed in her legs and her left arm. She also could not speak intelligibly. Her son made arrangements for Brian and his wife to talk to her through a video chat. Leanna described the experience:

"I'm talking to my mom, and I'm singing her songs, and we're doing LifeParticles. And all of a sudden my brother . . . he's saying, 'Oh my gosh, she just moved her left arm.' I said, 'What do you mean?' and he said, 'She just moved her left arm!'"

Brian and Leanna are convinced that the LifeParticles they sent made the difference. After that call, they kept her mother in their minds and sent her LifeParticles whenever they had a chance. After a month, the mother was moving her arm as if she had never had a stroke.

In their enthusiasm, Brian and Leanna are excited to share LifeParticles; they even did so with their cat, whose cancer went away after they kept sending him LifeParticles. Leanna exclaimed, "So then I got the huge belief in it. I want to send it all over the world. We can change the people; we can change the world. We just need to educate people, as many as possible."

Here is yet another story. Mingyeong Kim's mother, who is sixty-five years old, had spinal surgery but, ten months later, was having trouble recovering her energy. Mingyeong, who lives in another region, regularly opened her MindScreen and sent her mother LifeParticles. One day, she called her mother, whose voice sounded really strong. It was the most cheerful, energetic voice she had heard in recent days. When she asked why, her mother told her that a yellowish, bloody pus had poured from her nose and throat at the time that Mingyeong had sent her LifeParticles in a concentrated way. Her mother said that something that had caused blockage seemed to have come out. Afterward, even her lower back felt better, and she enjoyed great physical relief; she not only felt good, but also invigorated.

How are such things possible? Isn't it amazing that LifeParticles can be sent to people who are far away? Once you know the properties of elementary particles, you will be able to gain insight into such dramatic instances of healing.

It has been discovered that elementary particles can exist in more than one state or place at once. They can be spread over a wide distance and across physical barriers. Also, once two particles interact or bump into each other, they become "entangled," and their properties intermesh and become the properties of both particles. If you observe one, and then the other, they will always act as a pair or as twins. As you can see, our usual way of thinking in regard to space and distance does not apply to elementary particles.

Scientific observations teach us that the world is not

actually the way we see it and the world of the visible is not the only world. Because the entire universe came from a point where all components of the universe were present, and fused into unity, all beings and all particles of the universe are already entangled on the fundamental level. This means there are multiple layers of connections other than visible physical relations. Given this ultimate connectivity that encompasses the entire universe, wouldn't the mysterious action of LifeParticles being sent and received while transcending space be a real possibility?

Actually, we already know this through our own experiences. Haven't you felt something when a serious problem happened to your loved one even though they lived far away from you? Many people say that parents who are far from their children have nightmares or feel bad when their children are sick or something harmful happens to them.

I am sure most of you have had at least one incident of wondering or thinking about someone and, right away, or soon after, they call you, you run into them, or you hear about them from someone else.

You have access to information concerning people connected with you in the world of elementary particles. In that world, there are no secrets, and what you do clearly affects others. In the world of LifeParticles, physical distance presents no barriers.

Dr. Masaru Emoto, the previously introduced researcher who studied the correlation between information and water crystals, conducted this experiment. First, he photographed

A crystal of Tokyo's tap water.

A crystal of Tokyo's tap water after 500 people sent remote prayers.

crystals created with Tokyo tap water and found that clean crystals did not form, possibly because the water had been chlorinated. Then he put the same water in a bottle and placed it on top of his office desk. Next, he waited for an event to occur, something he had requested in advance from 500 people living all over Japan: at two o'clock that afternoon, they were all to fill their hearts with feelings of gratitude, wherever they were, to think that the tap water on the desk had become clean, and then to say, "Thank you." After that moment, Emoto immediately photographed crystals of that water. The photographs of those crystals were truly beautiful.

"Although we anticipated this," Dr. Emoto said, "concerning our obtaining such wonderful crystals, everyone on the photographing team was so deeply moved they couldn't keep themselves from weeping. The hearts and words of 500 people were transmitted to the water in an instant. Waves transcend space and time; so a thought occurring in my mind always affects the world. We hold in our hands the key to changing destiny."

If we make good use of the characteristics of such elementary particles, whose actions transcend space, and of the power of attitudes like love and gratitude, which can instantly send and receive positive LifeParticles, then previously unimaginable miracles could definitely happen.

Send LifeParticles to Your Loved Ones

Vanya Santa Cruz, who lives in Phoenix, Arizona, was working at her job in the summer of 2010. She was suddenly contacted by a hospital, and was told that she should come to the hospital and meet with a doctor immediately. Showing her an fMRI taken previously, the doctor told Vanya that a tumor had been discovered in her brain. Surgery was performed, but the brain tumor was not completely removed. Another fMRI was taken three months after surgery, but everything remained the same.

Vanya's father, Curt Hudson, wanted to take Vanya to where he had just moved, a place called Sedona, two hours north of Phoenix. Sedona is a city famous not only for its beautiful scenery of red rocks, deep blue skies, and wonderful juniper trees, but also as a place where a person can feel healing energy that is concentrated in areas called "vortexes."

They were walking the streets of uptown Sedona when they entered a store selling crystals and offering aura readings.

The person doing the aura readings looked at Vanya's aura photo and asked her, "Is there something wrong in your head?" She said she was worried that there might be a problem with Vanya's head, and recommended they take part in LifeParticle collaborative healing at the nearby Sedona Meditation Center.

Curt joined the meditation center and began participating in the LifeParticle collaborative healing every week, where, along with the other participants, he would send LifeParticles to Vanya in Phoenix. He also did LifeParticle Meditation on his own every day and sent LifeParticles to his daughter. Vanya visualized receiving those LifeParticles while doing LifeParticle Meditation. Vanya said that while she was receiving LifeParticles from the class or from her father, she could "feel a sort of a vibration, a tingly vibration over my body and I would feel—just hope and love in my heart. I would imagine LifeParticles coming down and it just made me feel just great."

Vanya also came to Sedona once and participated in a collaborative healing session herself. She had this to say about what she felt:

"It was an overwhelmingly emotional experience. It was just like being bathed in love, surrounded in love. I tingled from head to toe. I cried. The tears just came. They just came and came. I knew that this was what was going to get me through this."

Vanya slowly started to get better. Her once severe forgetfulness went away, she laughed more frequently, and she looked happy. They then took another fMRI. Her doctor gave her the results by telephone. With a voice full of surprise, he said that her brain tumor had disappeared.

She remembers that time well. "That it hadn't changed would've been the best news that I thought I would receive that day. I chanted that to myself because that was what I wanted to hear. I never, ever imagined that they would call me and tell me that it was gone."

It was truly a miracle! It was also a miracle that was hard for the doctors to believe and hard for her and her family to believe. Once you understand the nonlocal character of elementary particles, however, you realize that it was not, in fact, a miracle. It was a completely natural phenomenon. Although his daughter was living in a place two hours away by car, Curt's true love and earnest desire to see his daughter get better was delivered to her continually—transcending space—with LifeParticles.

Curt said, "Those people who think that LifeParticles or healing energy is not real, I very much wish that they would come and experience it, because it is real."

When you send LifeParticles with a true, honest heart like Curt's, when life energy is delivered in its utmost purity, then what we call "miracles" happen—for the world of the LifeParticles is a space of infinite creation where things happen as we determine.

When the person receiving LifeParticles, as well as those sending them, accept them with a true, earnest heart, their effects are doubled. Vanya said: "I think that having all of that healing, loving energy sent to me and experiencing it myself and meditating, I truly think that it was all of this. It was the

LifeParticles, it was all the love and healing I was getting from everybody. It was the love and healing I was giving to myself, and that's why the tumor has gone."

She added, "I want to work on myself and heal myself and get myself going. Also, I want to help people understand that they have that power themselves, that they can heal themselves, and that they need this life energy that comes to us. I want to help people heal."

Meditate with the LifeParticle Card

For people who are new at meditation, going into a deep meditative state can be difficult. I wanted to find a way that people could easily understand and experience the invisible world of LifeParticles, so I designed a quintessential representation of this world with an artist.

This image of the LifeParticle Sun is composed of elements of sacred geometry; the image resembles a round chakra, and it is composed of colors that can stimulate the body's seven chakras and charge them with LifeParticles.

The wavelengths of the light of the three primary colors that make up the image, in addition to white, as well as the different shapes, stimulate the brain in different ways. They bring your mind into alignment with the energy and consciousness of the LifeParticle Sun. The colors and the waves

and particles of the light reflected off the image also charge your chakras with LifeParticles.

The red circle in the center charges your first and second chakras; the gold color surrounding them charges your third and fourth chakras; the aquamarine and indigo colors filling the rest of the picture charge your fifth, sixth, and seventh chakras; and the white spread throughout the image changes your energy into a purer, more spiritual state.

Each color causes different bodily sensations and phenomena. Red brings powerful heat and vibration; gold brings love and healing; and aquamarine, indigo, and white bring spiritual realization and feelings of peace and unity. The colors and shapes of the LifeParticle Sun image are an effective and harmonious combination that evenly stimulates your seven chakras and charges them with LifeParticles.

I made this image into a card so that people could easily use it in their daily lives as they carry it around with them. I even named it simply—the "LifeParticle Card." The card is inserted inside the back of this book's cover for you to use right away. As a visualization of the invisible world of LifeParticles, this card contains special wavelengths that will help you to easily send and receive LifeParticles.

Let's look for a moment at the nature of waves. Everything in the universe is simply energy, and that energy vibrates at unique wavelengths. For example, electromagnetic waves can be divided into gamma, x-ray, ultraviolet, visible light, infrared, microwave, and radio waves. Of these, the part of the spectrum that we can see with our naked eyes is visible light. On the other hand, wireless devices like radio and television receive information through radio waves, which have long wavelengths and low frequencies. Radio waves have a range of frequencies, so when you want to listen to a particular broadcast, you need to tune the radio to the frequency of that particular station. Receiving LifeParticles works in a similar way. You have to tune your consciousness to the frequency of LifeParticles in order to receive them.

Radios have transmitters for converting the rapidly changing alternating current into an electromagnetic wave that can move through free space. Radios then transmit radio waves to us as sound. The LifeParticle Card could be called a "LifeParticle Transmitter" that has been created to enable anyone to receive and send LifeParticles clearly, quickly, and powerfully.

To receive LifeParticles, your consciousness has to enter a state that is capable of receiving them. The LifeParticle Card can help you to create such a state. By looking at the card, your consciousness will be able to easily pick up and resonate with the frequency of the LifeParticle Sun. Then you will be able to experience the energy emitted by the LifeParticle Card, which will enable you to turn on your MindScreen instantly. It's similar to how a door installed with a card reader opens automatically when the right card touches it. With the LifeParticle Card, you can switch to LifeParticle-level consciousness quickly. After opening your MindScreen, you can send LifeParticles to wherever or whomever you want just by visualizing the LifeParticles being emitted, like a laser beam, from the card.

The more you develop your skill and focus in this process, the faster you will be able to do it. Eventually, if you just hold a LifeParticle Card in your hand and close your eyes, you will be able to achieve a state of focused awareness in which you can send out LifeParticles within three seconds.

Feeling the Power of the LifeParticle Card

Let's try an experiment on the LifeParticle Card's effects with the one in the back of this book. Let's attempt to feel and charge your sixth chakra with LifeParticles coming from the LifeParticle Card.

With your spine straight and your body comfortably relaxed, hold the bottom of the card with one hand. Position the card about seven inches in front of your eyes, keeping your eyes open. Then slowly push the card to about ten inches away from your eyes, and bring it back to its original position. Repeat this motion for about twenty seconds as you concentrate on what you feel in your brain. You should feel a change in sensation inside your head. You might feel as if waves are coming into your brain from the card, or you might get a feeling of magnetism between the card and your head.

Next, stop moving your hand, position the card about seven inches in front of your eyes, and stare at it for about thirty seconds. Imagine the card transmitting LifeParticles through your eyes and optic nerve and into your brain, charging your brain stem, your Life Brain. You'll get a magnetic

feeling around and inside your brain, and you may feel as if some fluid is moving in your brain.

Now close your eyes and try to sense the feeling of LifeParticles filling your brain. Imagine those LifeParticles sinking along your spinal cord into the lower part of your body. Those with a highly developed sense of energy will be able to feel heat being generated in their lower abdomen and lower chakras.

You can use the LifeParticle Card for many different things—detailed instructions will be introduced later. Two of its main uses are sending LifeParticles to your own body and to others.

If there is anyplace in your body that is in poor condition, bring the LifeParticle Card to that spot and hold it about three to five inches away. Then imagine with your eyes closed the bright light of LifeParticles coming from the card and healing your body. If you continue to practice using the LifeParticle

Card, you will eventually be able to experience sensations like vibration, heat, electric current, and light as LifeParticles rush into your body. And, as your bioenergy field expands, you will feel as if you are inside a capsule of energy.

When you send LifeParticles to other people, you can touch a LifeParticle Card directly to their bodies; or, if they are far away, you can send them LifeParticles using the card on your MindScreen. When sending LifeParticles to someone spatially distant from you, put the card in front of your chest and turn it to face away from your body. Then turn on your MindScreen, display an image of that person on it, and imagine the bright light of LifeParticles being emitted to that person from the card.

Some Great Stories about the LifeParticle Card

I have been stunned by the stories of people who used the LifeParticle Card in diverse situations for various purposes. Their bountiful ideas and proactive mind are beyond my imagination, and I'm learning about creative uses of the card from them.

One woman, who lives in Washington, D.C., was traveling by airplane on a business trip to Paris. It was a long flight, and she found it very uncomfortable and disturbing to have to just sit without moving for so long. With nothing she could do and nowhere to run, she despaired over not being able to cope with the situation. Then she suddenly remembered that she was carrying a LifeParticle Card. She pulled out the card and placed it near her chest. When she connected with the LifeParticle Sun, and as she breathed deeply, she became calm and felt her body relaxing and growing warmer. She was incredibly grateful that this healing tool helped her to overcome her anxiety and tension for the rest of the flight.

Additionally, many people who sleep with a LifeParticle Card under their pillow or on their chest not only feel LifeParticles moving into and charging their bodies, but also feel that their bodies are lighter and their heads are clearer the next morning. You could also put a card on any part of your body that may be in poor condition and imagine LifeParticles entering and healing that place as you fall asleep.

One night, Naomi Boren of Atlanta, Georgia, was trying to fall asleep. Being sensitive to the energy in her body, she felt a lot of heavy energy in her chest that seemed to be stuck and wouldn't move, even with deep breathing. She tried tapping and pressing the area, hoping to release it, but, unfortunately, with no results. Instead, she felt intense pain and throbbing. Still calm, Naomi reached for the LifeParticle Card she kept on her nightstand and placed it on her chest. She reported, "The pain and throbbing immediately and completely disappeared! No joke, just like that!"

Lolita Crisostomo of Glenview, Illinois, was suffering from diabetes and high blood pressure from the strain of her job when she started doing LifeParticle Meditation. "I felt overwhelmed and burnt out from years of a hospital psychiatry practice," she said, "and decided on an early retirement."

Lolita also dealt with a painful keloid scar from a lateral mastectomy that was interfering with her daily life. When she learned LifeParticle Meditation, she would meditate on the LifeParticle Sun on the LifeParticle Card "to make it more effective," she explained. "Then I would even rub the card directly on my scar. Within about fifteen minutes, my pain lessened. Sometimes, it's better than ointment! I keep my LifeParticle Card in my pocket and use it daily to relieve my pain." Now Lolita's blood pressure and blood sugar are within the normal range—without medication.

Her husband, Antonio, who is also a psychiatrist, used LifeParticle Meditation when he was admitted to the hospital with severe abdominal pain from gallstones. He used the LifeParticle Card to meditate and massage his abdomen—and reduced his pain from a "10" to a "5." After working with LifeParticles, he and Lolita said, "We felt an increase in energy, improvement in sleep, concentration, positive coping skills, motor strength, and a decrease in pain and stress."

The Martinez family of Burbank, California, also started doing LifeParticle Meditation together, especially with the help of the LifeParticle Card. The two daughters, Maritza and Magaly, used the card on each other. When Maritza had leg pain, Magaly sent her LifeParticles with the card while massaging her leg with the other hand. Their father, Nacho Martinez, carries the LifeParticle Card in his wallet to relieve pain or anxiety quickly. He said, "When I am feeling anxious or fearful, I stare at the card while holding it in front of my forehead, then in front of the chest. I feel energy and calmness." Along with focused breathing, using the LifeParticle Card helped Nacho to calm down when he faced two panic attacks in two months.

Healing Communities with LifeParticles

People who have used LifeParticles to improve their personal lives are then often inspired to help their communities by forming Energy Meditation Circles. As of February 2013, there were about 3,000 meditation circles all over the world. As a result, LifeParticles are spreading out from a variety of places—including senior centers, community centers, schools, healthcare centers, workplaces, churches, and even homes.

One special meditation circle was started on Jeju Island in South Korea, which is called the Island of Peace. Sunhwa, a woman who runs a health center in Jeju City, is sharing LifeParticles with neighborhood people at senior centers and community centers in seven neighboring towns.

At one senior center, about thirty elderly people always eagerly await their ten o'clock class with Sunhwa, who is unfailingly full of laughter and passion. The moment she enters, their faces light up when they see her cheerful face. As they follow her exciting and fun-filled instruction, the seniors stretch, exercise, sing, and shake stagnant energy from their bodies and minds. At the end of the hour session, they close their eyes and hold their LifeParticle Cards while reciting this affirmation: "LifeParticles create miracles. My knees are getting better. I am the master of my body." Then they send LifeParticles with the LifeParticle Cards to areas of their bodies that are causing them pain, for example, their knees or lower backs. They also pair up and send LifeParticles to each other as they touch LifeParticle Cards to each other's bodies. From the bright smiles that spread across the faces of these seniors, Sunhwa says that she feels bright LifeParticles filling the senior center.

One senior says, "My right knee used to ache, but the pain went away after I did this training." Another says, "After I do this training once, my body feels much lighter and refreshed." Since witnessing the members becoming healthier and happier, town officials are also attending the class and experiencing LifeParticles; they have said they want to learn the method, and then later teach it to the townspeople themselves.

Sunhwa always does LifeParticle Meditation before leaving for class. Turning on her MindScreen, she brings up the townspeople and sends them LifeParticles. Afterward, when she arrives at the class, the programs for the day that are appropriate for their condition will actually come to mind. What is more, every day she opens her MindScreen and sends LifeParticles to the health center members she is managing, as well as to their families and friends. If, through her Mind-Screen, she sees people whose condition is poor, she sends them LifeParticles of love and healing. She does this until bright smiles spread across their faces on her MindScreen.

In case you are wondering, Sunhwa did not have some special ability from the very beginning. What she did, however, was practice ceaselessly with a LifeParticle Card. As a result, she now can read the state of health of a person who is far away and perform distant healing. When she holds a LifeParticle Card, she says, her MindScreen immediately turns on, and she feels the physical condition of the person shown on the screen. Early in the morning, or even when she's sitting in the passenger seat of a car, she holds a LifeParticle Card and sends LifeParticles to people. "I send LifeParticles to . . .," she says in her mind, imagining that LifeParticle light is being emitted like a laser beam from her LifeParticle Card.

Katherin Bledsoe, from Northern California, is one of over a thousand meditation-circle leaders in America and also cares for many people through her ten LifeParticle Meditation groups.

As a child, Katherin grew up under the care of a very compassionate caregiver; however, the woman couldn't speak very well because of multiple sclerosis. Katherin developed a deep bond with her and was one of the few people who could understand and interpret what she had to say. Since beginning LifeParticle Meditation practice a few years ago, she is always reminded of her caregiver's great compassion. That compassion motivated her to start leading meditation circles to share her love with others and, in the process, overcome her own obstacles.

Four years ago, she started her first circle at a senior community center. "At first, I was so nervous I couldn't comfortably stand in front of people," she said, laughing. Later, she became more confident. "Over that time, I had five to six people in the class, and now I have twenty to thirty and have expanded the class to six senior centers."

She started her second circle for retired nuns. Twice a month, about thirty sisters, mostly in their eighties, gather in a circle near the Sisters of the Holy Family motherhouse to participate in Katherin's meditation circle. They feel a lot of gratitude. "This is where I find the most peace," said Sister Jacinta Fiebig, age eighty-two, after a recent class. "I feel so fortunate to be able to do it two times a month."

"I love seniors so much," Katherin said. "We have to give back to them." Of the activities during the senior center meditation circles, one of her favorites is the heart-to-heart energy hug she gives each person at the end of a session, when she holds LifeParticles in her heart. "It's a beautiful moment in which the separation between two individuals dissolves. There are no words to express it; it is like souls connecting." Murthi Kalamangalam, an eighty-three-year-old Fremont, California man, said the embrace "is much more than a hug. There is so much kindness involved in it."

Katherin also uses the LifeParticle Card in an afterschool program she teaches. The kids look at the card and imagine what their goals are. Then she gives them paper and has them write down their goals. On Thursdays, she does another afterschool program at a school for the blind; every other Sunday, she leads a meditation circle at a relative's home for people in their twenties.

She and other energy meditation circle leaders are supporting one another and working toward a vision of creating brighter, healthier local communities as well as bringing greater joy to their own lives. They are a constant inspiration to me and remind us of the very nature of LifeParticles—and ourselves—that is *love*.

• • •

The light of LifeParticles is bright and brighter still;
there is no place it does not shine upon,
no place it cannot reach.

• • •

Become a Creative Observer

So far, I've introduced you to the basic principles of LifeParticle Meditation. In this chapter, I would like to talk
about how to maintain a positive state of consciousness just
by changing your perspective. This state of consciousness is
the ultimate goal of LifeParticle Meditation. Everything you
need for a fulfilling life springs from this consciousness, which
I call "creative observer."

When I was a child, I often thought, why am I here? About
the time the sun went down, I'd sit with my back to a bundle
of rice straw piled on the edge of a rice field, and watching the
stars rising in the darkness after sunset, I'd suddenly feel the
incredible immensity of space that is the night sky. Within
that space, my existence would suddenly feel strange—as if it
had come out of nowhere. I was plagued with thoughts like:

Why am I here now? Who am I? Where have I come from?

I existed in a cosmic space, where stars revealed their light one or two at a time on a dark background; and there was another me, who was aware of my existence and wondered at the reasons for it. There is me, and yet another me watching me. Haven't you had similar experiences? This is a form of self-awareness that most people experience, a consciousness that watches and is aware of its own existence.

In fact, you may be experiencing it now while reading this book. Are you aware that you are reading this book right now? Try to take a step back from that awareness. You'll feel a greater dimension of awareness, one that perceives you reading these words.

Seeing our consciousness is like looking in a mirror to see our physical selves. The being that is aware of me exists in a place beyond the self that I think of as "me." Consciousness can gradually expand its scope until the limited being called "me" completely disappears; what is left is pure consciousness itself, from which the distinction between subject and object has vanished. This is the consciousness of nothingness and the zero point that I have discussed in a previous chapter. The awareness that is watching everything from a centered place of complete unity, where everything is one, is the ultimate essence of who I am. That is the great life force of the universe, self-existent and eternal. It is "cosmic energy" and "cosmic mind," which I experienced at the end of my twenty-one days of ascetic practice.

I call that absolute, enlightened consciousness "the

observer." This observer is somewhat similar to the observer that is sometimes described in quantum physics. It's been shown in many experiments that the presence of an observer causes elementary particles to act as particles instead of a wave. The observer is not just a passive watcher, but a consciousness that has an effect on the world it perceives. To emphasize its active role as an observer and the creative power coming from that awakening, I often call it the *creative* observer.

The Way of a Creative Observer

A simple and important tip for becoming a creative observer is to be aware of the center of your brain and recover your zero point.

Try to be aware of your brain right now. Bring your attention inward to the center of your brain, even as you read this book, by remembering there is a consciousness in your brain that is watching you read. Being aware of the core of your brain in this way is a method for quickly switching your consciousness to the observer consciousness and feeling your life itself from the perspective of LifeParticles.

Switching to the consciousness of an observer preserves instant and long-lasting awakening. Awakening or enlightenment occurs in a moment. But it is not eternal. The place where we can find sustained enlightenment is in the observer consciousness that has recovered its zero point. Recovering observer consciousness enables you not only to experience momentary enlightenment instantly, but also to maintain enlightened awareness continually in your real life. Consequently, your practice and life won't be separate from each other.

The consciousness of the observer is the awareness that knows everything is made up of LifeParticles, and that all are one and eternal because of it. The creative observer is also the entity that can change and move those LifeParitcles at his command. I would say that even more important than being aware of yourself as LifeParticles is being aware that you are a creative observer who can move those LifeParticles to create and change.

The easiest states a creative observer can use her power to change are her emotions and energy state. Think about when you have been completely mired in emotions like anger or sadness. At such times, that anger or sadness may have felt like it was who you were. However, your emotions are not you, but yours; that is, something you have. Emotions drift by like clouds; they're not fixed and unchanging. If you are aware of your brain, recover your zero point, and watch your emotions with pure consciousness, you can clearly perceive your emotions as separate from yourself and that those emotions are an operation of particles your mind has created.

Once you escape from your emotions and enter a neutral state of consciousness, you can create what you want. Luckily, particles are not fixed; they can change their characteristics at any time, in accordance with received information. Your emotions, for example, flip-flop depending on what information is transmitted to your brain. To change your emotions to positive ones, then, give your brain good information. Instead of being lost in those emotions, input positive information and change your energy by moving your body, listening to music, or giving yourself empowering messages. You can make yourself joyful when you want to be joyful, sad when you want to be sad, and happy when you want to be happy. As a master of life with observer consciousness, you can play your different emotions—such as joy, sadness, and happiness—like a master violinist who creates and plays any music he desires.

If you watch yourself and people around you with the consciousness of an observer, you can clearly see that energy fields of their own making are dramatically influencing them. Anger, depression, anxiety, resentment, irritability—different thoughts and emotions create such energy fields. You hurt, worry, and are lonely, lost in the energy matrix you have created for yourself. What you need to do is clear away the energy field that is so heavy and troubling, and fill its place with LifeParticles.

This principle also applies to any harmful preconceptions or negative self-talk that normally occur in your brain. For example, let's say that you have ideas such as these: "I wasn't successful in the past. Nothing I do works out. It was that way in the past, so it will be that way in the future, too." Having very deep roots, those fixed ideas exert a great influence on your body and mind, whether or not you are aware of it. When you feel you are trapped in those negative ideas, concentrate your awareness deep inside of your brain, watch yourself from the perspective of an observer, and recover your zero point. Clear away the dark curtain of that negative consciousness and those fixed ideas that dominate and oppress you. And empower yourself with brilliant life energy coming from the LifeParticle Sun.

Once you take on an observer consciousness, your viewpoint of other people and the world will also change. When you view the world through observer consciousness, instead of analytic thinking that sees everything as separate individual beings, you awaken to the simple, yet clear, truth that all are one and united as vibrating LifeParticles.

Observer consciousness can become an effective barometer for checking the moment-to-moment state of your consciousness in daily life. Let's say that you are angry with someone, resent someone, or feel superior to someone. The fact that you have such feelings means that you are caught in a state of energy and awareness that draws distinctions and separates you from the other person. You cannot make use of LifeParticles in such a state. The instant you detect such a consciousness, try to switch into an observer consciousness. Try to recognize the other person as a vibrating LifeParticle body that is connected with you as one. In that moment, compassion and love will sprout in that place in your heart where there was once comparison, judgment, and resentment.

Concentrate your awareness deep inside of your brain, recover the zero point, and watch yourself from the perspective of an observer. Then try to draw on the power of the bright life energy that pours out from the LifeParticle Sun. This energy will change your attitude from negative to positive. Affirm it to yourself by remembering, "I am bright LifeParticles and a creative observer who can move those LifeParticles. I have infinite potential. I can create what I want in my life." Design your life anew with the creative power of LifeParticles.

Everyone has creativity. Creativity is not necessarily manifested only when you engage in some artistic activity, such as painting or dancing. Each and every moment of your daily life can be a moment of creation. Realizing that you stand at the center of the world, a center of creation, and moving LifeParticles to change yourself and change the world—that is being a creative observer.

Do you want to be a spectator, or a creative observer, a genuine master of your life? A spectator is just an onlooker who comes and goes without a sense of responsibility, but a creative observer stands at the center of her life and the world with a firm anchor. She is a master with a sense of infinite responsibility that comes from experiencing the essence of life and a deep love for the world.

When we realize that we are the real authors of our lives, we will stop blaming something or somebody else and take responsibility for our own lives. Then a true change begins. The power of your creativity will continue to be amplified when, using LifeParticles, you recover your physical and mental health, restore your personal relationships, and contribute to the world and to those around you.

I like Julie Gold's song "From a Distance." Her song reminds me of the world as seen through an observer's eye.

Seen from a distance, we are people in the same band playing music for everyone. We are artists who play the most beautiful instruments in the world—*life*.

When you are too close to something, you cannot see it fairly and objectively; you need to step away from it to see it whole. You can only look at something from a distance when you detach yourself from an obsession with your emotions and conceptions and go back to the pure zero point. Then you become a creator who does not merely watch from a distance, but who stands tall on the earth, "up close and personal," while changing yourself and the world.

The center of your life, the center of the world, is you and that place where you stand. Become an artist of life and change yourself and the world from that central place! Sing the song of your life and play its instruments! Continue to project on your MindScreen a picture of a future in which the sounds of each of our lives mingle as one to create a beautiful symphony of peace.

The Far-Reaching Effects of LifeParticles

I believe that an age of spiritual awakening and an age of widespread enlightenment could come if an awareness of LifeParticles spreads among all people. Many have been thinking that enlightenment is difficult and is something that only saints or special people can attain through very special effort.

The enlightenment of which I speak, however, is something

simple. It is realizing that "I am LifeParticles, and we are all LifeParticles. We are all creative observers who have real power to change reality." If you open your eyes as a creative observer and look at the world through LifeParticle consciousness, you are actually able to understand what the saints have been saying—that all are one. I am LifeParticles; you are LifeParticles; and the entire human race, the earth, and the cosmos are all LifeParticles. The dimension of oneness many saints and enlightened people have spoken of is not different from the dimension of oneness that vibrates as LifeParticles.

Once you know LifeParticles and awaken your observer consciousness, you understand that no spiritual leader or organization can monopolize spiritual awakening. The consciousness of individuals who have realized they are LifeParticles will awaken, and they will take responsibility for their own spiritual growth and enjoy their fill of spiritual freedom.

Worldly ideas divide people who live amid discrimination without even realizing it. Such concepts as the successful and the unsuccessful; the respected and the disrespected; the happy and the unhappy; the enlightened and the unenlightened; those who get applause and those who applaud; all reflect this mind-set. We are mired in the matrix of the material world, where everything seems separate from everything else.

LifeParticles, on the other hand, are the common denominator comprising all beings, transcending nations, peoples, religions, cultures, language barriers, and the gap between the rich and the poor. Though our ethnic backgrounds are different, and though our languages are different, we can communicate through LifeParticles and become one through LifeParticles. "May all be happy." This wish is at the heart of those who have experienced LifeParticles. Many of the man-made tragedies that we have experienced are due to the fact that so many people either do not want others to be happy or haven't yet realized that they don't have to sacrifice their own happiness for others to be happy. Can we really create such a world, a world where everyone is happy—and not where happiness for me means unhappiness for another, but where happiness for others means greater happiness for me?

It is indeed possible, but it will occur when everyone views the world through integrated LifeParticle consciousness— when hearts, bright like the sun, are revived within them. Put simply, a heart bright like the sun is the representation of a pure soul within, the divine nature within, or "conscience." From this, the sense of infinite responsibility arises, which is the realization that one's responsibility is not only for one's personal life but also for the general condition of humanity and our planet.

Einstein said, "May the conscience and the common sense of the peoples be awakened so that we may reach a new stage in the life of nations, where people will look back on war as an incomprehensible aberration of their forefathers."

Einstein's dream was not the dream of just one man. Countless people have the same dream and earnestly long for such a world to come. What are you dreaming of now? What kind of world are you drawing in your mind? Our future will unfold as we have drawn it. If we abandon the great dreams in our hearts as we draw a dark future stained by despair and misfortune, then the world will change, becoming just as we picture it.

Conversely, if we each draw on our own MindScreen a bright, warm world where everyone is happy and acts upon it, then the world will gradually change to take the form we give it. The futures that you and each one of us dream about will come together to create our world, and the world of the next generation.

I have hope for the future of humanity and our beloved planet. I believe you will feel the same hope when you experience the world of LifeParticles. LifeParticles bring out the ultimate goodness in you. If you can believe in yourself, then you can believe in humanity.

It's a transformative experience that words can hardly express when I observe the sun slowly peeking up over the horizon amid the stunning red rocks of Sedona, Arizona— where I live. All the darkness of the world withdraws when the sun rises in the morning and everything in the desert is granted new life. Today's new sun drives away the old darkness of the night to open a new day. The bright shred of sunlight is magnificent, and my heart and soul are touched, as I become part of a scene that has played out over and over again throughout millennia of earth's existence. It is one of the sacred moments that I cherish.

Remember, though, that we have the brightest sun in the heart of our being. We don't need to wait for tomorrow to see the sun. The LifeParticle Sun already, and always, lies inside of us. We just need to access the sun and let it shine through the world.

I imagine a world where people realize their true nature as LifeParticles and become creative observers who confidently change their own lives and the world.

In that world, we communicate through LifeParticles with a pure intention to help one another. We become LifeParticle Transmitters, sending, receiving, and circulating LifeParticles in every part of our life. In that world, we take charge of our own health and happiness and don't seek joy and bliss outside of ourselves. Our collective LifeParticle experiences will propel us to create a new way of living that is built on a complete oneness with everything. That will be a wondrous exploration for humanity, and the most amazing miracle we can create together with LifeParticles.

• • •

The person with a safe center doesn't fear change.
We can choose change without fear
only when we awaken to the center
where the observer consciousness,
our changeless self, resides.

• • •

Basic LifeParticle Meditation

I often compare the experience of LifeParticles to swimming and riding a bicycle. Just because you have a lot of knowledge about how to swim does not mean you can swim well. To know what swimming feels like, you have to get into the water yourself. The instant you sense the water's buoyancy, you get a feel for it: "Oh, so this is what it feels like!" Once you develop that feeling, swimming becomes easier, and you can really enjoy the pleasure and freedom that water gives. In contrast to this, for those who can't swim, water doesn't offer freedom. Instead, it is an object of caution, and one that can be very dangerous.

The difference between people who have experienced LifeParticles and those who haven't is actually similar to the above. When we are in the flow of LifeParticles, we can savor the joys of life, sending and receiving LifeParticles and creating our world to our heart's content; it's like swimming joyfully and freely in the clear, crystalline water of a limitless ocean. When we are not aligned with LifeParticles, we cannot taste the world of infinite creation that lies beyond the reach of knowledge and reason, because we tend to trust only our own knowledge and reason and are trapped within them. Hampered by caution and fear, we are unable to rise beyond them to the unknown realm of consciousness composed of LifeParticles.

To truly know LifeParticles, you have to experience them with every cell and nerve in your body; again, it's like learning how to swim. Information about LifeParticles can help you to understand them, but experiencing them directly is something quite different. The LifeParticles you are made of are not created by knowledge, thoughts, or ideas; they are the manifestation of life itself. Miracles and true changes cannot happen within the framework of thoughts and ideas. In that framework, you merely spectate and watch miracles happen to others.

That's why I say that LifeParticles are not learned, but "downloaded." Recently, we are seeing a flood of countless applications created for smartphones and tablet computers. The moment you install applications on those devices, they change into all-powerful machines with many amazing functions.

LifeParticle Meditation is such an application, or "app." Your body is a high-performance device, and LifeParticle Meditation is an amazing app that will not only bring you greater health and well-being, but will also help you create reality as you go back and forth between the conscious and unconscious worlds.

Just as you get a feel for swimming once you've experienced the buoyancy of water, the LifeParticle app is installed in you once you've experienced LifeParticles deeply. After the app is installed, you can easily enter the world of the unconscious to send and receive LifeParticles. Ultimately, like the longtime meditators who remain in a theta wave state throughout their daily lives, you can perform LifeParticle Meditation in any environment.

The most effective way to download and install the LifeParticle app is to use a card containing an image of the LifeParticle Sun. Try installing the LifeParticle app by using this image and filling your sixth chakra with bright LifeParticles. You can also do LifeParticle Meditation without the card by simply imagining the bright LifeParticles entering and filling your body.

Settings for LifeParticle Meditation

· · · ◉ · · ·

Setting up an ideal environment before beginning your meditation will give you a more powerful and comfortable experience. Here are some suggestions for you to follow.

Place & Time: Choose a quiet, secluded place where you can really focus on meditation. Anytime is fine, but it's effective to meditate, if possible, when your physical condition is good. It's best to meditate in the morning, when your head is cool and clear, or in the evening, after enough preparatory training to fill your body with vital energy.

Lighting: Use low-level lighting, because external light interferes with concentrating within yourself. Although it may seem a little dark at first, being in the dark is good for sensing the light of the LifeParticle Sun, which illuminates the third eye.

Posture: A full lotus or half-lotus posture is good for sitting meditation, but if you have trouble adopting these postures, you'll still meditate effectively sitting in a chair. If you sit in a chair, keep your feet parallel and shoulder width apart to form the number eleven, and keep your soles flat on the floor.

In a sitting posture, keep your spine and lower back straight to help energy circulate well in your chakras, which are arrayed along your spine. Relax your shoulders, chest, and arms, and put your hands palms up on your knees, either with your hands opened naturally or with the thumb, index, and middle fingers of each hand touching. Straighten your neck and tuck in your chin slightly. This is to minimize pressure on your neck and promote the circulation of energy to your brain. Close your mouth and touch the tip of your tongue to the roof of your mouth, enabling the energy to descend readily from your head, along your tongue, and into your throat. Gently close your eyes and smile slightly, which also facilitates the supply of oxygen and energy to your brain by opening the back of your neck and the base of your skull.

Preparatory Training: Awaken Energy Sensation

· · · ⊚ · · ·

If you are not yet able to feel energy, or have never tried it before, you should begin LifeParticle Meditation with developing your sense for feeling energy. To develop a sense of energy, straighten your spine while in a seated position. Place your hands on your knees and relax your shoulders, chest, and arms. Slowly inhale and exhale several times.

With your palms facing upward, slowly lift your hands from your knees and raise them to waist height. Concentrate your awareness on your hands. Visualize a brilliant pillar of light coming down into your hands.

As you concentrate on the feeling in the palms of your hands, slowly raise them about five inches, and then lower them to their original position. Repeat this motion slowly and continuously. Your hands will gradually become heavier as you feel a weight on your palms.

Now slowly bring your hands to the height of your upper abdomen. Turn your palms to face each other, leaving about two inches of space between them. Concentrate your awareness on the space between the palms of your hands.

Slowly move your hands apart so there is about five inches of space between them. It may feel as if they are pushing away from each other. Now decrease the space between your hands again, bringing them to about two inches apart. Do not let your palms touch each other. Repeat this motion slowly and continuously. Continue to concentrate your awareness on

your hands as you imagine the energy between your palms
gradually being amplified.

If you feel any subtle sensations at all in your hands, continue to concentrate on them. You might feel a sense of heat
or a tingling, an electric sensation, or a feeling of magnetism
or volume, as if you're holding a balloon between your palms.
These are all feelings of energy. Continue to repeat this movement and develop the magnetic feeling between your hands.

Five Steps of LifeParticle Meditation

· · · ⦿ · · ·

Step 1: Charging LifeParticles to the Brain

In a sitting posture, straighten your spine and lower back as much as you can. Imagine there is a line of energy from the top of your head down to your first chakra.

Bring a LifeParticle Card in front of your eyes. As you stare at the card's image, gradually move it to about seven inches away from your face, and then pull it back to about four inches. Repeat this movement as you continue to stare at the card for a while, and you'll feel something in your head. Keep concentrating on that feeling. Eventually, you will be able to sense magnetism between the LifeParticle Card and your brain.

Now hold the card still about seven inches from your eyes. Stare directly at the LifeParticle Sun image as you imagine LifeParticles entering your brain.

When you stare at the LifeParticle Sun, the feeling of magnetism may grow. Imagine light and waves of LifeParticles entering through your eyes into the center of your brain and into the brain stem, charging it with energy.

Step 2. Chakra Vibration

Now set the card aside and close your eyes. Focus on the feeling of LifeParticles filling your brain stem. Imagine them vibrating and moving quickly in your brain stem. The subtle vibrations there naturally cause your head to nod up and down rapidly.

If vibrations don't automatically happen in your brain, then nod your head up and down in short movements to get them going. If you continue to vibrate for a while, the rhythm of the vibration will begin to feel natural and automatic. Over time, you will start to vibrate unconsciously.

The vibration will send the LifeParticles in your brain stem downward, along the nerves of your spine, into your chest and lower abdomen. Call out, in your mind, "first chakra," to send LifeParticles there, and your first chakra a the base of the trunk of your body will vibrate powerfully. Once the energy in your first chakra seems to become active, shift your focus to your second chakra in your lower abdomen and sacrum and call out, "second chakra," in your mind. When your first and second chakras become active, you may feel heat and intense vibration in your hips and lower back.

Now concentrate, one by one, on the chakras in your solar plexus, heart, throat, and head; this will cause them to vibrate, and as they do, imagine the stagnant and heavy energy leaving each of your chakras.

After you have finished vibrating each chakra, if you have any particular place in your body that is in poor condition, call it to mind. LifeParticles will immediately move there, vigorously producing vibration and healing. If you continue to vibrate as you bring to mind, for example, organs or joints that are giving you problems, then old, unhealthy energy will leave those areas. The main purpose of this Chakra Vibration is to purify stagnant energy in each chakra, as well as the whole body.

Step 3. Chakra Breathing

After releasing old, unhealthy energy in your body through Chakra Vibration, practice Chakra Breathing for charging your chakras with healthy LifeParticles.

Here is how to do it. Slowly stop vibrating and straighten your spine once more. Relax the tension in your shoulders, chest, and arms. Rest your hands, palms up, on your knees, with the thumb, index, and middle fingers of each hand touching. Straighten your neck, and tuck in your chin slightly toward your body. Close your mouth and touch the tip of your tongue to the roof of your mouth.

Now use your breathing and visualization on your Mind-Screen to accumulate energy in your chakras with LifeParticles, beginning with your first chakra. Concentrate your awareness on your first chakra at the base of the trunk of your body. To gather energy more effectively, tense and contract your first chakra and anal sphincter. As you concentrate your awareness on your first chakra, display it on your MindScreen. Slowly begin energy breathing with your first chakra. Inhale as you imagine LifeParticles charging your first chakra with your breath, and exhale . . . inhale . . . and exhale.

As you breathe, imagine the chakra as a flower. Visualize its petals opening when you inhale, and then closing when you exhale. When the flower you picture gradually changes to an intense red, the energy rises along your spine to your second chakra. On your MindScreen, bring up your sacrum and the middle of your lower abdomen, where your second chakra is located, and slowly breathe with it. As you inhale deeply, push your lower abdomen forward; and as you exhale, pull your lower abdomen in toward your back. Visualize flower petals of a reddish-orange color in your second chakra opening up when you inhale, and then closing when you exhale. You will get gradually stronger feelings of heat as your lower abdomen is charged with LifeParticles.

Energy healing takes place as that heat spreads to your whole lower abdomen, which includes your kidneys, bladder, and reproductive organs. When the feeling of heat grows gradually stronger and your first and second chakras are sufficiently charged, you may also feel an ecstatic trembling as hot energy condenses in the chakras.

When your second chakra is full, that energy will rise along your spine to your third chakra. On your MindScreen, envision your solar plexus, where your third chakra is located. Do energy breathing with your third chakra. Continue to charge your third chakra with LifeParticles, imagining clear, orange-colored flower petals opening up when you inhale, and then closing when you exhale. As your third chakra is charged, the warm heat of LifeParticles will flow to your stomach and liver and heal them.

The energy of your third chakra now rises along your spine to your heart, your fourth chakra. Do energy breathing as you imagine your fourth chakra, shining golden and yellow, on your MindScreen. When you inhale, a golden flower opens, and when you exhale, the flower closes. As this happens, your fourth chakra is charged with golden LifeParticles. The bundles of negative emotion that have accumulated in your heart melt away with these golden LifeParticles. As it gradually grows warmer and more open, brilliant golden light spreads out from your heart.

The energy of your fourth chakra now rises along your spine and reaches your throat, your fifth chakra. Do energy breathing as you concentrate on your thyroid gland, which is located in the middle of your throat. Visualize a beautiful blue-green flower opening and closing with your breath. Imagine your fifth chakra being charged with LifeParticles as the intense, blue-green energy of healing spreads throughout your throat like the aroma of peppermint.

Your fifth chakra purifies the energy from your heart as it passes through. This purified energy then rises to your brain, your sixth chakra. Once in your brain, the energy moves around and heals every nook and cranny. As you watch the energy move on your MindScreen, you may notice areas of your brain that seem dark or blocked, and you may see them becoming brighter and more fluid as healing LifeParticles chase the dark energy away. As your brain gradually heals and brightens, a subtle smile may automatically spread across your face.

Now you're ready to welcome the LifeParticle Sun.

Step 4: Becoming One with the Light Particle Sun
Concentrate your mind on an indentation located just above the center of your eyebrows and imagine the LifeParticle Sun shining in front of your forehead. See light from the sun piercing your head through that point and entering your pineal gland in the middle of your brain. In a relaxed manner, and

with an open heart, continue to focus on that point in front of your forehead, and a kind of light will appear, piercing the darkness. All you have to do is wear a smile on your face and wait with a peaceful heart.

Deep breathing can help you maintain a sense of peace. Chanting short phrases in your mind, such as "The LifeParticle Sun" or "The LifeParticle Sun is shining on me," is also helpful for keeping your heart open.

Don't worry if you don't see the light during your first meditation. Usually, it takes time and many practices to purify and activate the energy in your sixth chakra in order for the third eye to fully see the light when your eyes are closed. Until then, just visualize the LifeParticle Sun image on your MindScreen or hold up the LifeParticle Card in front of your forehead, and you will be able to feel the magnetic energy of LifeParticles entering your brain.

The first light you may see when your sixth chakra is activated may be the color of aquamarine or indigo. It may appear small at first, but continue to focus on that light for a while and it will grow larger. That light is the LifeParticle Sun. Keep visualizing the LifeParticle Sun becoming brighter and shining on your brain, causing it to vibrate with LifeParticles. Your Life Brain awakens.

Now visualize the light of the LifeParticle Sun descending into your chest and healing your heart. Continue to accept that light with your heart. Open your heart even wider and welcome the LifeParticle Sun to your heart with a pure and grateful mind.

The light of life flowing out of the LifeParticle Sun keeps coming into you, rushing over you like blue waves as it heals your heart and fills it with love. You're being connected with the source of life. Accept its infinite, unconditional love; it is absolute, and one that you cannot receive from any other source. That light may even give you a kind of message. Try to hear that message.

The LifeParticle Sun is great love and blessing. It is the essence of life that you can feel directly. It is complete unity felt in a state of emptiness from which your ego has disappeared. Along with the words "Thank you," deep emotion may flood your heart, and your whole being may be in bliss with a new awakening. Enjoy your fill of the energy of love sent by the LifeParticle Sun. Gladness spreads across your face and through your heart. The boundary between you and the outside world disappears as your ego vanishes. Complete unity is being achieved in this empty state. Deep, genuine gratitude for your life fills your heart. The bright, warm light of the LifeParticle Sun is circulating now through your heart and body. You are now a small LifeParticle Sun.

Step 5: Visualize What You Want
With the feeling of becoming one with LifeParticle Sun, display on your MindScreen what you want and send LifeParticles there. Visualize the detail and outcome with all of your senses.

Summary:
1. *Charge Your Brain with LifeParticles:* Fill your brain

with LifeParticles from the LifeParticle Sun image.

2. *Chakra Vibration:* Following a natural rhythm of vibration, release old, unhealthy energy from each chakra, one at a time, from the first through the seventh.

3. *Chakra Breathing:* Breathe in and out of each chakra, from one through seven, while visualizing healthy LifeParticles charging each chakra.

4. *Becoming One with the LifeParticle Sun:* Breathe deeply as you picture the LifeParticle Sun in front of your forehead. Absorb its light until the inner light in your sixth chakra shines brightly and your body is filled with LifeParticles, bringing you feelings of joy, love, oneness, and peace.

5. *Visualize What You Want:* Project what you want to create on your MindScreen and send LifeParticles to it. Visualize the outcome with all of your senses.

The method I present in this book is the one I consider to be the most effective, not only from my own experience but also that of hundreds of thousands of other practitioners. At first, the LifeParticle Meditation might seem to involve many steps. However, when you get into the rhythm of the practice, each step unfolds automatically as a natural extension of the previous step. As you become more familiar with LifeParticle Meditation, you can create your own way of doing it—because, actually, there is no right or wrong way to do LifeParticle Meditation. Just simply thinking of LifeParticles with a good intention can also be a wonderful meditation.

Quick LifeParticle Meditation with the LifeParticle Card

··· ◉ ···

When you don't have enough time for meditation, you can perform a quick and simple method for activating each chakra using the LifeParticle Card.

Bring a LifeParticle Card in front of your forehead and use it to charge your brain with LifeParticles, as described previously in Step 1 (page 166).

Once you feel that your brain has been sufficiently charged with LifeParticles, bring the LifeParticle Card in front of your chest to open your heart. Visualize LifeParticles coming from the LifeParticle Card and opening your heart chakra. You may detect certain energy sensations, such as a feeling of energy moving in your chest, a sense of relief in your heart, or a feeling that your chest is more comfortable.

Next, bring the LifeParticle Card in front of your lower abdomen, visualize bright LifeParticles energizing your core, the second chakra, and feel your breath sinking deeply into your belly.

Now that you have charged your three main energy centers, energize each chakra, one by one, starting with the first, by bringing the LifeParticle Card in front of it. The power coming from the card will easily activate each of your chakras. After charging all seven chakras, you could also open up the energy points in your head with the LifeParticle Card. Send LifeParticles wherever you think there are blockages in your head—the sides, front, back, or base of your skull.

Next, visualize becoming one with the LifeParticle Sun as described previously in Step 4 of the LifeParticle Meditation (page 170). If you can't yet see the light of LifeParticles with your eyes closed, bring the card in front of your forehead and visualize LifeParticles coming out of the card and into your brain. With a bright, comfortable smile on your face, imagine that sun shining on you with bright LifeParticles and sprinkle LifeParticles all over your brain, face, and chest.

Use the card to send LifeParticles to parts of your body that need healing, to another person, or to a situation you want to manifest.

c h a p t e r 12

Meditations for Manifesting What You Want

While you can send LifeParticles to anybody in any situation, or for any outcome you are able to imagine, here are some common purposes for which you may want to send LifeParticles during LifeParticle Meditation, once your MindScreen is open and you are filled with LifeParticles.

I've included instructions for meditations, which you can modify for your own needs, and affirmations that will add the power of your voice to your meditation.

However you choose to use them, remember to sow the seed of your desires and dreams on your MindScreen and nourish them with LifeParticles until you manifest them in the physical world. This art of manifestation needs constant practice and sincere effort. Once you master this art, you become the driver of your destiny.

Healing Your Body

··· ◎ ···

In addition to creating an optimal energy state in your body—Water Up, Fire Down—which is crucial for overall health and well-being, you can use LifeParticle Meditation to alleviate a health problem by picturing that part of your body on your MindScreen and imagining LifeParticles of love and healing surrounding and penetrating it.

First, display your body on your MindScreen and scan it with your mind's eye. In a state of awakened energy sensation, you might see a possible dark spot or a problem. You may also feel, rather than see, the issue. If a part of your body feels tight, painful, or uncomfortable, then those places need healing.

The next step for healing is to release the unhealthy, stagnant energy from your body. To release the old energy, Chakra Vibration, as described in Step 2 of LifeParticle Meditation (page 166), is very powerful and effective.

After sufficiently releasing the old energy, visualize the painful part of your body on your MindScreen and send bright, healthy LifeParticles there. Although you can send LifeParticles using just your visualization alone, it can be more effective if you use the LifeParticle Card. Take a LifeParticle Card, hold it about two to three inches away from where you're hurting, and send LifeParticles there. Visualize bright LifeParticles being emitted from the card to your body and healing the area.

You can say, "I'm sorry" to those places, sharing your regret for having failed to take care of them and causing them to suffer. Then share your heart by sincerely caressing and loving the places where you hurt while saying, "I love you."

Imagine those parts of your body being healed by the light of LifeParticles as dark, heavy energy withdraws from them and they become healthy and glowing with vitality. Tell your body, "LifeParticles are now healing every part of my body," as a smile spreads across your face and gratitude fills your heart.

Now put down the LifeParticle Card at your side and rest your hands on your knees. Visualize the LifeParticle Sun above your head and imagine you are in a pillar of bright LifeParticles coming down from the LifeParticle Sun. When you inhale, imagine LifeParticles entering and filling your body; when you exhale, imagine LifeParticles healing the painful part of your body, releasing the dark energy there. LifeParticles are entering each and every one of your cells, healing your body as they vibrate. The deeper you breathe, the brighter and more numerous the LifeParticles coming into your body will be.

Finally, picture yourself becoming rejuvenated and enjoying walking, running, or doing your favorite activities without pain or discomfort. Healing is taking place according to the images displayed on your MindScreen. The more specifically you visualize, the more effects you can experience.

Give thanks with these affirmations:
"LifeParticles are healing every part of my body."
"I am blessed and thankful for my perfect health and vitality."
Keep repeating this process daily until you are completely healthy and content.

Face-to-Face Healing

··· ◉ ···

Use the following method for someone who is physically present and wishes to receive LifeParticles:

Have the other person, the LifeParticle receiver, sit or lie down. A sitting posture is no problem for advanced meditators, but lying down helps with stabilizing brain waves. It also helps to relax beginners and others who find sitting uncomfortable or who are in poor health. When lying down, have the receiver spread their feet shoulder width apart and their arms slightly away from their sides, with palms facing up.

As the receiver closes their eyes and continues to exhale through their mouth, encourage them to relax and stabilize their brain waves through motions such as shaking their legs or bouncing the backs of their knees against the floor. Once they are relaxed, have the receiver slowly stop moving and open their eyes.

Now hold a LifeParticle Card about five inches from their eyes. As you tell them to concentrate on the image of the LifeParticle Sun, repeat the movement of slowly raising the LifeParticle Card to about seven inches from their eyes, and then lowering it back to about four inches. Next, coach the receiver to imagine LifeParticles entering their brain. They may get a feeling of magnetism between the LifeParticle Card and their head. Have them close their eyes when they get such a feeling, while they continue to imagine LifeParticles spreading to their whole body through the spine.

Now hold one or two LifeParticle Cards close to the person's chest and heal the energy in their chest. Imagine bright, powerful waves of LifeParticles coming from the LifeParticle Card(s) and entering the receiver's chest. Tell them to focus on the feelings in their chest.

If the receiver has a specific place in their body that is in poor condition, bring the LifeParticle Card(s) to that location and send LifeParticles there for a while. Focusing light with a magnifying glass onto a piece of paper generates heat, which causes physical changes in the burning paper. Similarly, if the healer sends LifeParticles with their whole heart, and the receiver accepts those LifeParticles with an open, focused mind, the receiver's energy changes and also leads to chemical and physical changes. Phenomena associated with those changes are feelings of vibration, heat, or seeing bright light.

At this time, the receiver may feel some vibrations in the targeted area. Vibration is a natural phenomenon when LifeParticles penetrate blockages in the energy pathways. If vibration naturally occurs, tell the receiver not to resist any automatic vibration. Instead, tell them to move according to what they feel. If vibration doesn't occur, you can help them to maximize the healing effect by leading them to vibrate; for example, say, "Now your knees vibrate. Keep vibrating your knees. Healing is happening in your knees." After the vibration has quieted, have the receiver stop moving, inhale with a deep breath, and then exhale. Then, one more time, bring the LifeParticle Card closely to that area and charge it with LifeParticles for a while.

Adding the visible vibration to the healing is optional, not mandatory. Although the effect of vibration is powerful, if you don't have enough confidence to do it, or the receiver doesn't feel comfortable about it, just sending LifeParticles with the card and your sincere heart is sufficient. Healing also happens through energetic vibrations that are invisible to the eye.

After you finish LifeParticle healing, have the receiver take a few deep breaths and open their eyes. Ask them to talk about what they felt and also share what you experienced. You'll both realize that what the two of you felt was very similar.

At the end of the session, state these affirmations for them:
"Your body is full of healthy LifeParticles."
"You are healthy and whole."

Distant Healing

To help someone with LifeParticles at a distance, picture them and their issue on your MindScreen. If they don't have a particular issue and you just want to send them love, just picture them. If some part of that person's body is in especially poor condition, expand it on your display; or you can scan them the way you scanned your body (see "Healing Your Body," page 178) and check on how they are doing. You'll get a sense for the person's condition if you display his or her physical and mental state on your MindScreen while holding a LifeParticle Card.

Now imagine LifeParticles of love coming down to you from the LifeParticle Sun above your head, into your heart, and out to the heart of the person you want to help. If you want to use the LifeParticle Card, hold it over your heart chakra with the image facing away from you. Imagine LifeParticles being emitted from the LifeParticle Sun on the card and going to this individual.

In your mind, say, "I send LifeParticles to (their name)," and emit LifeParticles at the same time.

Imagine LifeParticles of love healing the places where they hurt. Visualize the dark, unhealthy energy in that place leaving their body as their body becomes bright and glowing with vitality. In addition, transmit bright LifeParticles to the person's heart chakra to open their heart. Shine the bright light of LifeParticles on them so that the energy troubling them can leave their heart, and fresh, bright energy fills it. With all of your senses, feel that they are happy and healthy and have all they genuinely desire.

Next, visualize sweeping and healing their aura with bright beams from the LifeParticle Card, and create a protective LifeParticle capsule around their body. See them glowing brighter and brighter inside a capsule of light as they smile at you with gratitude.

If there are more people to whom you'd like to send LifeParticles, bring their images to mind and use the same method. Send them plenty of LifeParticles of love until their faces are cheerful and smiling.

Afterward, say the affirmation:

"Don't worry. Everything will work out for you. A bright, warm capsule of LifeParticles is protecting you."

Recharge from Fatigue

· · · ✦ · · ·

As we go through our daily lives, our energy becomes easily drained. We lose our concentration, we start to drag, and our mood takes a turn for the worse. At times like these, recharging with bright LifeParticles will help you to recover.

With your back straight, close your eyes and, as you breathe and meditate, bring up your MindScreen. Imagine the LifeParticle Sun shining brightly above the crown of your head and bright LifeParticles pouring down from it and into your body. Your mind will grow clearer and more refreshed if you imagine LifeParticles pouring into your head like a waterfall, rinsing and cooling it.

Next, imagine that LifeParticles are sinking into your chest and that your heart is filling with loving LifeParticles. If you continue to breathe as you visualize these things, your chest will feel more comfortable and your breathing will deepen. Now imagine LifeParticles sinking from your chest to your lower abdomen. If you continue to breathe deeply into your abdomen, it will grow gradually warmer with vitality. After charging your head, chest, and lower abdomen with LifeParticles, in that order, imagine the brilliantly shining LifeParticles filling your whole body.

Another way to charge yourself with LifeParticles is to use a LifeParticle Card. Hold a LifeParticle Card and bring it in front of your eyes, then use it to fill your chakras with LifeParticles. After absorbing the red color in the card with your lower abdomen, the golden-yellow color with your heart, and the indigo color with your brain, imagine a bright aura of LifeParticle light surrounding your whole body. Once you're charged with LifeParticles, your face will grow brighter as your heart opens up and a smile forms on your lips.

Add these affirmations:

"Bright LifeParticles are energizing my body."

"Every cell in my body vibrates with energy and health."

Changing Habits

The first tip for changing undesirable habits is to charge your body with the vital energy of LifeParticles. Those who have a great deal of blockage in their heart chakras, such as when they are bored, lonely, angry, or under stress, also experience a decrease in the bright, healthy LifeParticles in their bodies; consequently, they feel a stronger need to fill that lack or emptiness with energy such as that from food, tobacco, or alcohol. When you feel those cravings, charging with bright LifeParticles helps regulate those needs related to bad habits. If you have enough life energy charge, you will become able to calm and control your emotions more easily.

The second tip for changing habits is turning on your MindScreen and doing some image meditation. Instead of obsessively thinking, I absolutely must not do this, try imagining yourself becoming free from that habit on your MindScreen. The power of the imagination in the unconscious world is greater than that of the will in the conscious world.

For example, let's say that you have a habit of binge eating. Instead of forcefully restraining yourself when you see food, turn on your MindScreen and picture yourself calm and smiling as you look at the food in front of you. Motivate yourself by visualizing yourself changed when you don't binge on food, and see your family and loved ones rejoicing with happiness for you. To free yourself from unwanted habits, visualize yourself having successfully changed your habit and send it LifeParticles. Play out your new actions as if they were real, and ready yourself for real-life situations. Keep taking concrete actions to change your habits. Daily LifeParticle Meditation is an effective way to regularly reflect on your actions and make any necessary adjustments to your action plan. Remember that being consciously aware of how you are doing with your resolution plays a significant role in changing any habits.

Be determined—but also be kind to yourself. Do not punish yourself with self-hatred, even though you keep falling again into the same old habits. Go back to the zero point with LifeParticle Meditation, renew yourself, and try it again until you get there. Every day is a new day and every moment is a new moment, no matter what you did before.

Add these affirmations to your meditation:
"My heart is full of bright, warm LifeParticles."
"I have the power to change my life."

Improving Personal Relationships

$\cdots$ ◉ $\cdots$

There will be people whom you've hurt or people who have hurt you, and there will be people you dislike or who dislike you without any particular reason. Personal relationships that aren't harmonious are like holes through which your energy leaks. You waste your energy worrying uselessly about relationships with those people, or whenever you think of them, negative rather than positive energy is created, which makes your energy dark and heavy. That is why restoring all those personal relationships that you think of as uncomfortable to their original, natural state is not only good for you but also good for other people.

First, use a LifeParticle Card to charge your brain so that it and your whole body are filled with bright, pure LifeParticles. Bring up on your MindScreen a person with whom you want to restore a personal relationship. Waves of emotion connected with that person, such as hate, resentment, or regret, may rise up in your mind. Bring the LifeParticle Card in front of your chest and heal the emotional energy in your heart chakra. When you exhale, discharge from your mouth the energy of the emotions in your heart. Purify your emotional energy as you continue to heal your heart.

Once the energy is purified to a certain extent, close your mouth and slowly control your breathing. Then turn on your MindScreen and watch the other person with the consciousness of LifeParticles. Using the LifeParticle Card, send

LifeParticles to the person as you watch them with a heart free of emotion, that is, zero-point consciousness.

Remember that you are LifeParticles and the other person is LifeParticles, too. The emotions of hatred and resentment will melt away as the realization dawns on you that you and they are one at the level of LifeParticles. You are one. How could you hate or resent them? Send the other person LifeParticles containing the pure love and compassion that arise from deep within your heart with an attitude of prayer so they will truly realize that they, too, are LifeParticles.

Imagine the other person's body and face gradually becoming brighter and clearer through LifeParticles as their heart is also healed. And say this to them:

"You are brilliantly shining LifeParticles. I am also LifeParticles. We are one at the level of LifeParticles."

Send LifeParticles to the other person with a smile of reconciliation, forgiveness, and love. If there is anything you want to say to the other person from your heart, share it with them. For example, you can say, "I'm sorry," "Forgive me," "Thank you," and "I love you."

The deeper the emotional scars in the relationship, the more you need to repeat this meditation to clear away the emotional waves that are troubling you.

If you run across the other person in your daily life, try to view and interact with them with the consciousness of an observer. You're looking at yourself, as well as the other person, from the level of LifeParticles. Once you realize that you are LifeParticles and they are LifeParticles, you will gradually be able to speak, act, and express yourself naturally.

Conclude your meditation with these affirmations:

"I am loving and kind toward myself and others."

"(Person's name), you and I are one as LifeParticles."

"(Person's name), I respect you. I send you LifeParticles of love."

Envisioning Your Future

If you want to manifest your future as you imagine it, what you should first examine is your answer to the question: What exactly do you imagine?

What future do you imagine for yourself? In it, are you healthy, successful, and happy, or not that happy, and worn out by life? The brains of many people may, unconsciously, be full of worries about the future as they imagine themselves exhausted by life, rather than imagining happy futures for themselves.

If you want to manifest your future as you imagine it, then you must begin by clarifying what it is you are imagining. What do you want, exactly? A good, healthy figure? Attractive friends of the opposite sex? A healthy family? To change your habits? Material plenty? Success and prestige? A life of spiritual growth and sharing?

I would suggest picking the future that would most satisfy your heart. A rule of thumb is: The simpler your goal, the better. If you have a large dream, breaking it up into smaller steps can help you visualize and accomplish it. Once you achieve what you have chosen, you can set up your next goal.

Envision LifeParticles going to a picture of you successfully achieving your dream or goal. Rather than only picturing the end result, see yourself going through the process of completing it, and imagine how you will feel once it is finished.

For example, if you have to give a presentation in front of

people, or if you have an important sporting event coming up, try experiencing it virtually in advance on your MindScreen. Imagine the audience and all the individuals involved, and then visualize everything happening in great detail, just as you want it, and just as if it were completely real. Lastly, imagine yourself smiling—and those around you smiling and congratulating you—about the successful completion of your project. As you continue to imagine a good outcome, repeat to yourself, "I can do it," or, "This work is already done." This is pulling forward a picture of a good future and showing it on your MindScreen. You can also send LifeParticles to the people who will play an important role in realizing your dream.

Use as much detail as you can and fill the images with LifeParticles. This picture on your MindScreen is a hologram created by LifeParticles. The more you concentrate your awareness, the stronger the bright LifeParticles will grow.

Continue to practice this meditation on your MindScreen until your brain completely believes it is a fact. When powerful information is input into the brain within the unconscious, the brain just accepts it, because it is unable to distinguish between whether it has happened in reality or in the imagination. The picture of you on your MindScreen and your affirmation are also information. When your brain perceives that information, electrical and chemical signals are generated in its synapses, transmitting the information from neuron to neuron and spreading the effects throughout your body. All of your cells, as well as your brain, start to accept what you have imagined as fact.

Once changes of consciousness and changes of information affect your whole body and brain in this way, your energy also changes, which affects your will and attitude toward life. Thus, the power of LifeParticles, augmented through MindScreen meditation, becomes a potent driving force that enables you to move passionately to create what you want in reality.

If you would like to create the future you want, fill yourself with LifeParticles through MindScreen meditation and continue to realize each event, one by one, through the power of those LifeParticles. Once you know how to draw the infinite energy of the cosmos and to use LifeParticles in your life, then your future has already become a reality! Continue to empower yourself until you have achieved your goal.

Add these empowering affirmations to your meditation:
"I know I can do it."
"The work is already done. I am grateful for its success."

Filling Your Space with LifeParticles

Filling places like your room, home, office, and desk with better energy will have a positive influence on your life. Space is not empty—it is filled with vibrating particles, which are continually influenced by their environment. Let's see how you can fill your own space with the good energy of LifeParticles.

First of all, you need to get your spaces clean and in good order. If your room is messy and dusty, it means you have shown little care for that space. Cleaning our rooms has the effect of clearing out old energy from that space, but it simultaneously has the effect of cleaning our minds. When you clean your room, the worries and emotions you have piled up in your heart are cleaned along with it. Thus, your refreshed mind is able to fill your room with positive LifeParticles.

Try rearranging the objects in your space, or decorating it so that it generates better energy. For example, decorate your room so that it gives you the brightest, most comfortable, and warmest feeling possible. During the day, open your windows appropriately so that bright light enters the room; bring in plants that absorb hazardous substances and supply oxygen, moisture, and negative ions; and hang wall art or place crystals that give off good vibes. If you meditate or pray, prepare a small space where you can do that in one area. It's also good to hang an image of the LifeParticle Sun in that space, or anywhere you want to transform the energy into the light, love, and unity the LifeParticle Sun represents.

Put your true heart into meditation and prayer. Draw in the life energy of the universe, visualize your body filling with bright LifeParticles, and then spread that light out from your body to infuse your space with shining LifeParticles.

The more you do LifeParticle Meditation, the greater the concentration of LifeParticles in your space will grow. Then those who enter it will feel, and may say, "Wow! The energy here is great!"

After meditation, say these affirmations aloud or in your mind:

"This space is full of LifeParticles and positive energy."

"My space is always filled with joy, peace, and love."

"My space supports all of my dreams and brings abundance to my life."

Loving Your Pet

Most of us can't help but love our pets. They are adorable beings that are dependent on us. We can talk to them like a friend or smother them with heartfelt love like a child. Because our pets accept and give love without calculation or discrimination, our hearts naturally open more easily when we're around them. Sometimes it's easier for us to use the energy of our heart chakra and develop it by raising a pet than it is in our relationships with other human beings, who are more complicated and self-protective. As beings of love, however, humans naturally want to share it with others. Feeding, petting, cleaning up after, and talking to our pets help to prevent our heart chakra energy from stagnating and turning into loneliness.

We can also use LifeParticles to care for our pets. Sending them to our pets helps them to be healthier and full of love. To send LifeParticles in a concentrated way, calm your mind and body when the pet is sleeping or resting. Bring a LifeParticle Card close to its body and imagine LifeParticles going from the card to the pet. Face the palm of your other hand toward the pet and imagine LifeParticles are being sent from there as well. Six energy channels, including the heart meridian, go through our hands, which are directly connected to the heart chakra. That's why loving energy is shared directly through the hands when we touch someone or send them LifeParticles.

Start by sending LifeParticles to the pet's head, and

then move down to its chest, belly, and legs. As you visualize LifeParticles entering the pet's body and making it healthier, say out loud or in your mind, "I love you!" After sending LifeParticles, keep the LifeParticle Card slightly away from the pet's body and use it to sweep through their energy field from head to toe. Imagine the stagnant energy in its body leaving from its toes and its overall energy becoming brighter and clearer.

Tell your pet:
"Thank you for being here with me."
"The love I receive from and give to you enriches my life."
"You are always healthy, happy, and whole."

Caring for Your Plants

··· ◎ ···

Raising plants is another practice that causes joy to quickly well up in the hearts of many people. Plants, of course, provide us with oxygen and share the unaltered, pure energy of nature. What's more, air-filtering plants eliminate hazardous substances such as benzene, formaldehyde, and trichloroethylene. NASA has published a list of such plants.

Not only do the green leaves and stems of plants purify our air, but even one plant left in a room gives us more of a feeling of being in nature. In watering and feeding a plant, making sure it gets the right amount of light, and wiping down its leaves, we can taste the joy of caring for another living organism. Just as the title character in Antoine de Saint-Exupéry's *The Little Prince* was grateful and happy for the one rose he cared for and loved on his planet, and considered it to be more precious than the thousands of roses he discovered on the earth, we can form a close personal bond with the plants in our life. I am always moved by the awesomeness of life when the plants that I have prized and grown from seedlings finally bloom and open their brightly colored petals, one by one. I wonder, entranced, where in the world do these beautiful colors come from?

The joy and benefits we receive from raising a plant can be amplified when we commune with our plants through LifeParticles. To do this, look at the plant with your eyes and your MindScreen. First, take in the plant overall. Imagine it in its pure state—as an aggregate of vibrating LifeParticles, rather than something solid. By doing this, we are sending it energy. Some people might even see the energy field, or aura, around the plant being activated. It may look brighter, fuller, and larger.

Next, we can use our MindScreen to look carefully into its leaves and petals. Sense the mystery and wonder of life in their colors and patterns. Connect your heart to what you see and speak what flows out of you in response. I often say, "You are really beautiful. I love you." Just as in the onion experiment, our plants receive pure, loving energy from positive words spoken from an open heart. Speaking to a plant recognizes it as a life-form that is readily influenced by energy. When we do this, the energy connection between the plant and us grows stronger.

Now bring a LifeParticle Card close to the plant and imagine LifeParticles going to it. Visualize the energy of love in your heart chakra going out through your palms to the plant as well. Imagine the plant receiving the LifeParticles and the vibration of the LifeParticles in the plant becoming more vigorous.

After giving it what you feel is plenty of energy, you can, in turn, accept pure energy from the plant through your palms. Imagine energy overflowing from the plant to your palms and into your chest. Closing your eyes and visualizing this for a while will make it stronger. Do this until your energy field and that of the plant become linked as one. Then it is possible to feel the life energy of the plant healing your heart chakra and spreading throughout your body.

As you imagine the body's energy field being healed by the pure energy of nature, tell the plant that allowed you to have this experience:

"I appreciate your bountiful beauty."
"All is well with you. Thank you. I love you."

When you have less time, you can also briefly send loving LifeParticles to your plant at any time of day, especially in those short moments when you water it. It is also beneficial to place a LifeParticle Card by its pot, or put a sticker of the LifeParticle Sun directly on the pot.

Communing with Nature

When we find it challenging to circulate our body's energy on our own, we can receive nature's assistance by opening our heart and mind to the natural world. Nature will open our energy points and breathe life energy into us.

During pleasant weather, look at the sky without focusing your eyes; you will be able to see swirls of light filling the sky and rotating so fast they cannot be identified. These swirls are energy pouring down from the sky to the life on earth. You can gather them into you by closing your eyes, straightening your back, and concentrating on the crown of your head to open your energy point there. Then you can imagine those swirling energies entering your head, chest, and lower abdomen, releasing stuffy energy and filling you with fresh energy.

Vibration or different kinds of bodily motions may manifest naturally at this time in the process of releasing stagnant energy. Stand with your legs shoulder width apart and make your mind and body comfortable. As your energy channels open, your body may rotate, stretch, or shake however it is inclined. Allow it to move freely, and concentrate on the body's sensations to help the energy circulate everywhere inside.

When the vibration calms, the energy purification is done to a certain extent. Now sit, calm your breathing, and visualize a line of LifeParticles stretching from the crown of your head to the bottom of your trunk. When pure, bright LifeParticles enter the crown of the head along this line of energy, see them filling your head, chest, lower abdomen, and each of your chakras. Concentrate on your body's feelings and try to feel your whole body vibrating and filling with LifeParticles. Then you can open your eyes and look around slowly while you are connecting to what you see. If there are trees nearby, you can choose one and examine it closely. Try to see the tree as vibrating with LifeParticles, or see the aura around the tree. Say to the tree, "How are you?" Send it loving LifeParticles from your heart. In return, the tree is likely to transmit the pure LifeParticles of nature as well. Accept these LifeParticles into your heart chakra and continue to communicate with the tree from your heart. This loving exchange can balance and strengthen the heart chakra, making you feel more peaceful and grateful.

You can also communicate with nonliving things in this way. Try it with mountains, rocks, and water. With this communion, you can feel unity with what is around you and renew yourself with the support of nature.

Say to the natural world around you:
"I am grateful for the life you give me."
"I heartily thank you for your infinite blessings."

Healing the Planet

Our planet is the home of humanity and of all our fellow living and nonliving residents. So, when we send LifeParticles to the earth, our healing intention and benevolent mind reaches humanity and everything on this earth. Sending LifeParticles to the planet is a great way to experience the loving nature of LifeParticles, transcending all illusory borders and separations.

Turn on your MindScreen and display before you a little picture of the earth. Look at our beautiful planet with a loving heart. With your heart, accept the light of the LifeParticle Sun above your head and send LifeParticles of love toward the earth.

Bring your hands close to the planet and imagine that brightly shining LifeParticles from your hands are healing yourself and the earth. You can strengthen the experience by holding LifeParticle Cards in your hands and sending LifeParticles to the earth. As it is healed by LifeParticles, the earth gradually starts to glow a bright blue.

Imagine more and more people realizing that they are LifeParticles, and picture them awakening to the fact that they are interconnected at the level of LifeParticles. Imagine people exchanging LifeParticles of love, giving them to and receiving them from one another; imagine people being happy as their consciousness grows brighter. Picture the earth and all its inhabitants being healed and thriving.

State these affirmations:

"I trust the ultimate goodness of humanity."

"Our planet earth is becoming healthy and whole."

"May peace and love prevail on earth and in humanity."

Daily LifeParticle Meditations

Once you've practiced the basics of LifeParticle Meditation for a while, try to expand your LifeParticle experience into different parts of your life.

LifeParticle Meditation is based on universal energy principles. Thus, if you get a sense of how these principles work through your own experience, it is easy to apply the same principles to other areas of your life.

You can use LifeParticle Meditations and the LifeParticle Card at different times of the day: in the morning, while working or eating, in the evening, and even while sleeping. In this chapter, I introduce ways you can use LifeParticles in your daily routine. It will help you to constantly energize yourself and stay in a good energy condition "24/7."

Morning Meditation

The dazzling sun rises every morning, and we welcome a new day. Darkness slowly fades from the black expanse of heaven, and the blue sky reveals itself. Why not also welcome the sky on your MindScreen at these times? If you quietly open the crown of your head and meditate as you accept cosmic energy in the early morning, you can experience the LifeParticle Sun shining as the indigo-blue sky unfolds before you. In the tranquil hours of the morning, you can easily enter a meditative state because your brain waves are relatively slow.

Sitting with your lower back straight, welcome the light of the LifeParticle Sun by doing either the five steps of LifeParticle Meditation or quick LifeParticle Meditation with the LifeParticle Card. Breathe for a while with your eyes closed, and invite a light like the indigo-blue sky before your eyes. That is the LifeParticle Sun and the life energy of the universe. The LifeParticle Sun will wake up your Life Brain, and your eyes and brain will gradually grow clearer and brighter. Accept that pure, unadulterated light, and let it sink into your chest and lower abdomen. Once your chest and lower abdomen are charged with bright, warm LifeParticles, a deep sense of gratitude will automatically arise within your heart. Then you may hear a voice of awakening or, perhaps, a feeling in your heart that communicates the following:

"Today, I offer my thanks for permitting me to have this precious life for another day. I can get up this morning, breathe, and welcome the blue sky and the Sun on my MindScreen, all thanks to the life energy of the universe. Even now, through my breath, through my beating heart, LifeParticles ceaselessly enter my body and maintain my life. Communion with the life energy of the universe is a great expression of love and a blessing. My life, my day, are miracles—indescribable manifestations of love. In gratitude for this day, I will make the best use I can of the precious life energy given to me, always thankful and sharing love far and wide." In this way, get up in the quiet hours of the morning every day to align the energy of your body and mind, and do meditation for welcoming the daylight. Let LifeParticles come down into your head and your heart, and become one with the essence of life itself.

Once you are sufficiently charged with the light of the LifeParticle Sun, you can bring up images of other people on your MindScreen to send that light to them. Visualize yourself smiling brightly as you share LifeParticles with those around you. Imagine shining LifeParticles pouring from your face through your warm smile and the light of your eyes, and imagine those around you becoming brighter and happier as they accept the light flowing from you. If you let the LifeParticle Sun rise in your heart every morning, its warmth will radiate from your chest, and your day will be better for it.

Affirm to yourself:

"I am the LifeParticle Sun. The bright, warm LifeParticle Sun is shining in my heart!"

"Today I will share the best of myself with the world."

Workplace Meditation

No fine work can be done without concentration. It is especially essential for people who work or study while sitting down for long hours. The clearer, more refreshed, and more optimal the condition of our mind, the more our concentration increases. The condition of our mind is essentially and inseparably connected with the condition of our body and energy system. Our heart chakra should be open so that our mind is bright and positive, and our body's energy circulation should be smooth so that our head is clear and our lower abdomen is warm.

The LifeParticle Card has a superior effect on increasing concentration by putting the mind in optimal condition through smooth energy circulation. Many workers and students say they have increased their concentration with a LifeParticle Card and, as a result, have improved their learning or work performance.

Let me introduce several ways to use the LifeParticle Card.

First, when you want to instantly improve your concentration, use a LifeParticle Card to augment your brain power. Holding a LifeParticle Card in one hand, bring it in front of your eyes and stare at the image of the LifeParticle Sun. Imagine shining LifeParticles entering your brain from the image on the card. If you repeatedly bring the card closer to your forehead and then move it farther away, you'll get a sense of magnetism developing between the card and your head. Imagine that the stronger the feeling of magnetism grows, the more the power of your brain is augmented.

If you want to experience amazing concentration, begin your work or studies after increasing your brain power with LifeParticles in this way. What's more, your understanding, memory, planning ability, creativity, and other brain functions will improve dramatically.

The second way involves placing a LifeParticle Card on your desk in a clearly visible location to receive a charge of LifeParticles continuously as you work or study. If you use a computer, set the LifeParticle Card right next to the computer screen. Imagine LifeParticles contantly entering your body while you're working or studying. If you do this, your mind will grow bright and positive as you feel LifeParticles charging your whole body and brain, and you will focus better as your mind grows clearer and freer of distracting thoughts.

The third way is to use a card for recovering your concentration and energy level when they have dropped. When you feel low on energy, get up and move instead of continuing to sit in your seat. Energy blockages develop in the hips when you sit for a long time, because they are the part of the body that is folded in your chair. It's good at such times to get up and walk for a bit. If you refresh yourself by stretching, stepping outside for some fresh air, or getting some energy through healthy food, the flow of energy in your hips will become smooth and, as this happens, the fire energy that had gathered in your brain and chest will sink. Once the heat in your head has cooled to a certain degree, return to your seat and do LifeParticle Meditation.

You could increase your brain power by using a LifeParticle Card to charge yourself with LifeParticles, or you could do the following meditation for charging your whole body with LifeParticles:

Set up a LifeParticle Card on the desk in front of you and spend some time receiving LifeParticles as you stare at the image of the LifeParticle Sun. Straighten your back and close your eyes. Visualize LifeParticles pouring down into the crown of your head from above you. Imagine brightly shining LifeParticles continuing to fill your brain, and your brain shining brightly. As you imagine this, your face as well as your brain will grow brighter, and you'll smile without even realizing it.

Next, imagine LifeParticles descending from your head into your chest and filling your heart chakra. You'll feel your breathing growing easier as your chest becomes more comfortable. Continuing, imagine LifeParticles going down from your chest into your lower abdomen. As the vital energy fills your lower abdomen, your core, you'll feel your breathing sinking deeply into your belly. Your mind will become calmer and more grounded if you just breathe a few times with your consciousness focused in your core.

Once your energy is balanced and centered in this way, open your eyes and resume your work or studies. Even after this, try to maintain this good energy state for as long as possible as you imagine LifeParticles emanating from the LifeParticle Card and charging your body.

When at work, many people have a tendency to focus only

on what they're doing without realizing the condition of their body and mind. Moreover, they are unaware of their posture while they are engrossed in their tasks. Bent postures, such as crossed legs, or the head and neck pushed forward toward a computer screen, obstruct energy circulation. If such conditions continue, fire energy rises to the head, heating the brain, and causing a marked decline in concentration. Additionally, tension accumulates in the body and the ability to control stress deteriorates. As a result, a person is easily stressed, even by the little irritations that surround them. A straight back with uncrossed legs, on the other hand, allows energy to circulate adequately in your body, keeping your head clear and cool and allowing your mind to concentrate well.

Don't forget your body and mind while you are engrossed in what you're doing. Instead, through LifeParticle Meditation, practice being aware of your physical and mental energy state and your breathing while you work. Then the efficiency of your work/studies will improve amazingly through your much better energy condition and concentration.

After meditation, affirm to yourself:
"My mind is clear and focused all the time."
"I know I can do this."
"The universe supports all of my efforts."

Healthy Eating Meditation

··· ◉ ···

Mealtimes can be a good time for meditation. Instead of hurriedly eating, simply to relieve your hunger, why not use meals as a time for meditation? If you do that, your meal will become an opportunity to watch yourself and feel the life within you three times a day. Below I introduce four tips for LifeParticle Meals.

First, send LifeParticles to your food. Before eating, turn your palms toward the food and imagine LifeParticles coming from your hands and filling the food with healthier, more vital energy. You might even hold a LifeParticle Card in the palm of your hand. Try to connect energetically with the food that will soon change into a part of your body. If you understand that the food you eat is a precious resource that will become your body's energy, blood, and cells, you will automatically look for fresh, healthy food. Whenever you eat, a good attitude to have is: The life energy of this food makes my body healthier and more energetic.

Second, savor the food as much as possible. Notice its colors, shapes, and smells; as you consume it, focus on the flavors and textures in your mouth. While you do this, your consciousness turns inward, and you feel the life inside you more easily. Focusing on TV, a newspaper, or a book at mealtime requires care because your consciousness is externally focused. Instead, your meals will now become a form of meditation because your distracting thoughts will decrease, and you will focus solely on your own life phenomena.

Third, chew your food thoroughly. You've probably heard that chewing your food well is good for your health. It allows your saliva to break it down more efficiently and makes digestion an easier job for your stomach. It also makes you feel more full because, after ten to twenty minutes of eating, you feel more satiated, regardless of how much you've consumed. On top of these benefits, chewing your food about thirty to fifty times gives you the chance to experience it and focus on it in detail. One trick is to put down your silverware after each bite, or at least set down the hand that is holding the silverware, and resist the urge to pick up more food until you've swallowed.

Fourth, concentrate on your core. While you are eating, focus on your core, the lower abdomen, and imagine the food's life energy filling it with warm, vital energy. By concentrating your awareness on your core, you can not only enliven your consciousness back to your body, but also help the fire energy of your head and heart to sink to your abdomen. Thus, while eating, you can experience a state of meditation—a state of Water Up, Fire Down—with a cool head and a warm belly.

Affirm to yourself:
"I give thanks to the life energy of the food I'm eating now."
"LifeParticles from the food I'm eating nourish my whole body."

Evening/Sleeping Meditation

Since sleep not only allows our bodies to produce bioenergy and recover from fatigue but also allows our minds to process the complicated information obtained during the day, it is important for it to be of good quality.

Evening meditation can help guarantee this by purifying your information and energy. Of course, some preparations are necessary. This involves relaxing your body from the day's tensions and releasing its accumulated stagnant energy. Eliminate blockages and discharge stagnant energy through stretching and exercises. Cleaning your body with warm water is also helpful for clearing the stagnant energy away.

Create a dimly lit environment in a quiet, secluded place. Sit with your back straight, and imagine that your body is putting down roots into the earth. Place your hands lightly on your knees and gently close your eyes. As you feel your body, consciously relax all the tension within it.

Genuine meditation is a state in which all distracting thoughts have vanished; what is more, it is a state in which you are unaware that you are even meditating. The best method for eliminating any distracting thoughts is concentrating on the breath. Do Chakra Breathing; begin with your first chakra, and then concentrate, in sequence, on each chakra for a few minutes. You'll be able to concentrate more effectively if you emit LifeParticles to each chakra with a LifeParticle Card.

After charging your seven chakras, you might reflect on

your day; set up a plan for what you have to do the next day; and send LifeParticles to those parts of your body in poor condition or to other people.

By entering an unconscious state through evening meditation and purifying and clearing away the day's complicated information and stagnant energy, your fatigue will be easily relieved and you will enjoy a good night's sleep. What's more, when you meditate the next morning, you will definitely feel that the energy of your body and mind has grown clearer and more transparent.

It's very important to meditate in the mornings and evenings. Take even ten minutes to empty your mind of distracting thoughts and to watch your breath flow in and out. Make the habit of cultivating your body and mind as important as taking a shower and brushing your teeth. If LifeParticle Meditation becomes a habit, you will develop a powerful energy center that will make your energy more grounded and rooted, and the quality of your days will definitely improve.

Even if you do LifeParticle Meditation before going to sleep, you can continue to experience the beneficial effects of LifeParticles while you're sleeping with a LifeParticle Card. All you need to do is put one or more cards on or under your body or under your pillow. Many people have seen improvements by doing this.

For example, twelve-year-old Magaly, who has ADHD and lives in California, used to sleep in her parents' room because insomnia would keep her awake at night. Since she started placing a LifeParticle Card under her pillow, however, I was told that she sleeps well and gets up only when her parents awaken her in the morning.

When you're lying in bed, placing a LifeParticle Card directly on your body is even more effective than keeping it under your pillow. Turn the card so that the image of the LifeParticle Sun faces your body. If you place it on your chest, the energy of your heart chakra will be activated. You will be able to feel your chest growing more comfortable and your breathing deepening and becoming more stable. Sensitive people can feel the healing energy of LifeParticles moving in their chests. This healing phenomenon is clearly different from what you feel when you only focus your consciousness on your chest without using the LifeParticle Card.

Place the LifeParticle Card just below your belly button to fill your core with LifeParticles. With LifeParticles going into your lower abdomen, your energy will become more grounded and Water Up, Fire Down energy circulation will be stimulated. Your breathing may deepen, and you may be able to sleep more peacefully.

It's fine if you fall asleep with a LifeParticle Card on top of or underneath your body. Try to go to sleep feeling that LifeParticles are healing your body and filling it with healthy life energy while you sleep. When you get up in the morning, you will really be able to feel that your body and mind are much lighter and more refreshed.

Affirm to yourself:
"I give thanks to everything that came to me today."

"(Your name), you did a great job today. I love you."

"During the night, my body and mind will be fully rested and charged with LifeParticles."

"I will wake up light and fresh tomorrow morning."

Q & A about LifeParticles and Their Application

You might still have some questions about LifeParticles and how they work. I hope the answers to these questions frequently asked by LifeParticle Meditation practitioners around the world clear up any confusion you may have.

One important thing that I want to emphasize once again is: Do not try to analyze. Feel and experience LifeParticles for yourself. Then you will naturally discover the truth of the LifeParticles inside of you.

Remember, LifeParticle Meditation is like swimming or riding a bicycle. It is an art you learn and master through actual experience, not through intellectual knowledge. Consistent practice can deepen your understanding of LifeParticles and their application.

On LifeParticles

1. Are LifeParticles something you've newly developed that didn't exist before?

LifeParticles are not something I've developed that didn't exist in the world before. Before I named them, LifeParticles were a natural phenomenon. I merely rediscovered a phenomenon that already existed and organized the principles by which it operates in a way that anyone can understand and use in their daily life. In my desire to help people live happy and healthy lives, and to create a brighter world together, I used LifeParticle principles to develop LifeParticle Meditation, the LifeParticle Sun image, and the LifeParticle Card, so that people can bring their consciousness to the level of LifeParticles rapidly and send and receive LifeParticles effectively.

2. Are there good LifeParticles and bad LifeParticles like there are good energies and bad energies? Are the LifeParticles I feel through LifeParticle Meditation special?

LifeParticles themselves are neutral or pure. They are neither "positive" nor "negative," "good" nor "evil." However, LifeParticles carry information. With your consciousness, you can impose what could be called "positive" or "negative" information on LifeParticles. For example, if you want to send positive LifeParticles to your friend, by focusing on your intention with a bright and positive mind and sending LifeParticles with that intention to them, you are encoding those LifeParticles with "positive" information, which is then carried to them. What changes LifeParticles is none other than information, or consciousness.

Because LifeParticles are pure, they have the power, like clean water, to purify everything and restore a natural state. When your consciousness, through LifeParticle Meditation, recovers its zero point and enters the world of pure, bright life, you will be able to experience those pure, bright LifeParticles. That is the energy of unconditionally pure, great love, bliss, and healing felt through unity with the source of life.

3. Are LifeParticles always entering me, whether or not I perceive them? Or do they enter me only when I recognize them and concentrate?

Not only are you yourself LifeParticles, but right now, even at this moment, LifeParticles are ceaselessly entering you. Through the food you eat and the air you breathe, through the energy points in your body, countless LifeParticles are entering your body and supplying you with life energy. LifeParticles come into you even when you are not aware of it. Even death doesn't change the nature of LifeParticles. It only changes the way LifeParticles act upon you.

Although LifeParticles are always coming into us, we can receive brighter and more vital LifeParticles, and more of them, by elevating and focusing our consciousness. LifeParticle Meditation is a way to do this. Once you're connected with the LifeParticle Sun through LifeParticle Meditation, you can charge yourself with the energy of pure, bright, infinite life, and you can use and send LifeParticles where you want through your MindScreen.

On the LifeParticle Card

1. Is the image on the LifeParticle Card the same one you see during meditation?

I can't say that the image of the LifeParticle Sun on the LifeParticle Card is completely identical with the light seen when the sixth chakra is activated during meditation. The color, size, and form of the light seen, which differs from person to person, depends upon their personal experience and degree of meditation experience. Generally, at first, indigo or aquamarine colors are seen; later, this brightens to a dazzling bright light. You may have an experience in which the light seems to approach you, or in which you seem to follow the light and enter its space.

I created the image of the LifeParticle Sun after thinking long and hard about how I could help people easily understand and experience the unseen world of LifeParticles. This visualization enables you to encounter a feeling that is similar to the feeling of the LifeParticle Sun received through meditation when your sixth chakra is activated.

What's important is the feeling you actually get through the image. The special wavelengths coming from the shapes and colors of the image will help you to charge your chakras and bring your mind to a zero-point consciousness. This combination enables you to feel more peaceful and possess greater vitality of body and mind.

2. Do I definitely need the LifeParticle Card when I do LifeParticle Meditation?

No, you do not need the LifeParticle Card to do LifeParticle Meditation. However, you can charge your chakras and feel energy much more quickly and intensely if you meditate with a LifeParticle Card. You will be able to feel the difference clearly if you try meditating both with a LifeParticle Card and without one.

You could do a simple test right now. Try feeling your body's energy state with your eyes closed and without looking at a LifeParticle Card. Next, while looking at the card, charge the chakras in your brain, chest, and lower abdomen with the LifeParticle Card. Now feel your body's energy state with your eyes closed. Have you ever been able to feel more powerful energy?

The LifeParticle Card is a "LifeParticle Charger" that rapidly and powerfully fills the chakras of busy modern people who live in a fast-paced information society. It's also a "LifeParticle Transmitter" that can be used to send and receive LifeParticles effectively.

3. I placed a LifeParticle Card on my desk. If I just leave it like that, will LifeParticles automatically come out of the card?

As spoken of in sacred geometry, all shapes, colors, decorations, and structures have their own unique energies. In the same way, the shapes and colors of the LifeParticle Sun also emit specific energies. Therefore, just placing a LifeParticle Card somewhere causes it to affect the energy field surrounding it.

Your self-awareness and consciousness are important for receiving that energy more powerfully, however. Once you place a card somewhere, there is a big difference between not paying attention to it and being conscious of the image and receiving LifeParticles from it. The power of the LifeParticle Card feels very different to different people, and one's perception of this depends upon the consciousness with which it is used. Some understand it merely as a sort of image, while others actively use the card in their daily lives to charge themselves with LifeParticles and to send LifeParticles to other people.

LifeParticles are created by the power of your mind and are perceived through your senses. The degree to which you can feel bright, powerful LifeParticles using the LifeParticle Card will be amplified in proportion to your ability to concentrate.

On LifeParticle Meditation

1. I don't see the LifeParticle Sun when I do LifeParticle Meditation. Do I have a problem? What should I do at times like these?

You don't need to be disappointed or worried because you don't see the LifeParticle Sun. Some people have a developed visual sense—while others don't. Even if you don't see it as a visual image, you could feel the LifeParticle Sun in some other way, like a pulsing, whirling energy, for instance. There is no need at all to be concerned or impatient about it.

Even those who, at first, don't really see the LifeParticle Sun will see it sooner or later, once their senses are sufficiently opened and prepared. The LifeParticle Sun is visible when the energy of the sixth chakra is activated. In order for that to happen, the chakras below it must first be activated. When the lower chakras are cleansed, pure energy must naturally rise to awaken the sixth chakra.

Concentrating only on the thought of seeing the LifeParticle Sun never helps. When you concentrate only on your thoughts, your energy gathers in your head, hindering your natural energy circulation and balance and, in serious cases, resulting in a headache.

Rather than concentrating on the mental image of the LifeParticle Sun, you should awaken your body's overall sense of energy through stretching, breathing, and/or meditation.

You especially need to activate the energy of your heart chakra. The best way to activate your heart chakra is to feel gratitude. Try to recognize and be grateful for even the small sensations of energy you feel in your body. When the energy of gratitude and sincerity sufficiently fills your heart, it rises to your head naturally, enhancing your senses and other brain functions.

When you have trouble seeing the LifeParticle Sun during meditation, bring up on your MindScreen the image of the LifeParticle Sun that is on your LifeParticle Card. Imagine the light of LifeParticles pouring into you from the LifeParticle Sun. You could even bring the LifeParticle Card directly in front of your forehead or chest and charge your sixth or fourth chakra with LifeParticles. Whether or not you can clearly visualize an image of the LifeParticle Sun, what's important is connecting with the energy of the LifeParticle Sun at the very moment that you are conscious of it.

2. I got a headache during LifeParticle Meditation after I continued to focus on my brain to see the light of the LifeParticle Sun. Why do I get a headache? What should I do when that happens?

As I mentioned previously, the light of the LifeParticle Sun naturally becomes visible after your lower chakras are sufficiently charged and your sixth chakra is activated by their energy. The reason you got a headache is that you focused on your brain, your sixth chakra, when your body and mind were not sufficiently relaxed and your energy was not adequately activated in your lower chakras.

Energy easily gathers in the brain, especially in modern people. All day long, we live surrounded by computer screens, emails, text messages, and many other forms of information. Also, if you have a lot of thoughts and worries, your brain operates without resting, making it difficult for your body and mind to relax comfortably in a state emptied of thought.

For those who get headaches or who have trouble concentrating because they have a lot of thoughts, it is essential to relax your body and mind comfortably and get your energy circulating by doing enough preparatory exercises. Stretching or some dynamic exercises such as Brain Wave Vibration, which open the body's blocked meridians, and preparatory training for awakening energy sensation in your body, will help with this. It is also very important to purify and charge all of the body's chakras by repeatedly focusing especially on Steps 1, 2, and 3 of LifeParticle Meditation.

There are cases, though, when a person does enough preparatory practice and still gets a headache. In this situation, the headache can be a natural healing phenomenon that occurs in the process of energy being healed in the sixth chakra. There are many energy points in the head. If energy starts to circulate in the brain through meditation and many of them are blocked, a headache may develop in the process of those energy points opening up. This is a natural occurrence of healing, so you don't need to worry about it. It helps, at such times, to continue discharging stagnant energy from your brain as you relax your body and mind, and exhale slowly, but forcefully, through your mouth while making the sound "Hooo..."

3. I felt heat in my body when I did LifeParticle Vibration. Afterward, I experienced my body growing cold. Why is that?

LifeParticle Vibration generates heat and stirs up the old and stagnant energy in your body. Stagnant energy can have different characteristics, but it is often cold, wet, or heavy. The warm energy generated drives out cold energy, allowing warm energy to circulate in its place. Thus, you may feel cold when cold, stagnant energy leaves your body. This sensation is a good sign that cold energy is being de-cluttered in your body. If cold energy gets stuck in your organs or joints, warm energy cannot flow there, which reduces energy circulation and causes disease.

The tips of your fingers and toes, in particular, are major exits for departing stagnant energy; after vibrating, it's good to shake out your arms and legs and focus on the tips of your fingers and toes to allow cold energy to leave more easily. Another good method for expelling stagnant energy is lying comfortably on your back with a LifeParticle Card on your lower abdomen and visualizing cold energy leaving through your fingers and toes.

When you feel cold after doing LifeParticle Vibration, it's good to warm the inside of your body by drinking hot water or tea. Once cold energy leaves your body to a certain extent, your energy circulation will improve further, and you will be able to feel your body growing warmer.

4. After doing LifeParticle Vibration, my body hurt more, but then, later, felt better. Why is that?

There may be times when your body hurts temporarily after doing LifeParticle Vibration. You may also experience other symptoms, such as feeling heat, cold, or nausea. These are generally healing signs that occur as the body is purified of stagnant energy. Accumulated stagnant energy inhibits smooth energy circulation.

As you remove that energy by stimulating it with LifeParticle Vibration, you may feel pain. This pain will disappear of its own accord. Once it is clear, your body may feel much lighter than before.

The principle is similar to how a person feels muscle pain more intensely than usual on the day after they exercise. Although you feel pain, your muscles are actually rebuilding themselves. In the long run, your body will feel stronger and healthier. In the case of energy, your energy system is refilling itself with fresh, healthy energy.

When you experience such healing effects, your ability to handle the pain and your energy vitality will be enhanced if you store energy in your lower abdomen through deep breathing as you relax comfortably without moving your body too much.

5. I want to focus quietly on breathing and awareness when I do LifeParticle Meditation. Do I have to vibrate whenever I do meditation?

Vibration is one of the fastest methods for circulating energy. The purposes of vibrating when you do LifeParticle Meditation can be divided into two general categories.

The first purpose of vibration is to heal your energy when you're not feeling well physically. Your energy is healed when LifeParticles enter a part of your body in poor condition and heat and vibration are generated there.

The second purpose is to create the energy state most conducive to meditation by rapidly activating the energy of your chakras when you do LifeParticle Meditation. When your chakra energy is activated, the energy circuits in your body allow for good circulation, which lets you easily enter a meditative state.

However, you don't necessarily have to vibrate if the energy state of your chakras is good enough; if so, you will easily be able to activate your energy simply by breathing and concentrating your awareness on each chakra. Another way you could activate each of your chakras is by using a LifeParticle Card, as in quick LifeParticle Meditation, instead of doing Chakra Vibration.

Doing Chakra Vibration is generally effective for healing as well as for LifeParticle Meditation. However, since it is not absolutely necessary, I recommend that you choose an approach based on your own energy state.

On LifeParticle Healing

1. When I send LifeParticles to other people, should they know about it in advance or should I just do it without their knowledge?

LifeParticles are an operation of consciousness. Consequently, they act more powerfully when two people concentrate than when one person does. When both people concentrate in the same way, greater resonance develops as the frequency of the consciousness of the person sending LifeParticles unites with the frequency of the person receiving them. Thus, when you send LifeParticles to someone far away, explain LifeParticles to them in advance and set a time for distant healing. At that time, have the person receiving LifeParticles visualize them entering their body and healing it as they focus on their body in a relaxed and comfortable way.

Using the LifeParticle Card can further increase the effectiveness of this practice. The person doing the sending visualizes LifeParticles being emitted from the LifeParticle Card and going to the other person. The person doing the receiving can place a LifeParticle Card on the part of their body that hurts; at the same time, as that part is being healed, they can visualize stagnant energy leaving through their fingers and toes.

After the distant healing is done, it's also good to share what you felt during the healing. This will let you confirm the principle that energy follows where the mind goes. You will both feel that your minds and energies are interconnected in the unseen world.

2. When you send LifeParticles to another person, is it effective even if the other person knows nothing about LifeParticles and has no prior experience with them? What should you do then?

Even in cases where you are prevented from explaining LifeParticles to the other person in advance, LifeParticles will still be effective if you send them. LifeParticles will be shared with the other person to the extent that you focus and put into them the energy of a sincere, devoted heart. After sending LifeParticles, if you later talk to the other person, explain how you sent LifeParticles and tell them about the principles of energy. Then make plans for the next experience, at a time when you can concentrate together to make it more effective.

In those cases where the other person really cannot accept the idea of energy, especially in the sense of healing, just keep sending LifeParticles with a sincere heart. Energy is bound to go where the mind focuses. It's important to send energy with sincerity and conviction and also with the certainty that, one way or another, the other person will end up feeling it.

There are times when the situation makes it inappropriate or impossible to tell the other person. You could also send LifeParticles to someone you don't even know. For example, you could convey your energy of deep concern, compassion, and love as you think about people on the other side of the globe who are suffering because of some massive natural disaster.

If the situation permits, send LifeParticles after you inform the other person in advance. Never forget, though, that the LifeParticles you send can reach anyone, anywhere, at any time, even if they don't know about it.

One mother, Antonia Ortega, of Las Vegas, Nevada, tried this with her daughter using LifeParticle Cards. She was a typical teenager who was passing through a rebellious period. Continually angry, she would scream at her mother, refuse to clean her room, and never do what her mother wanted her to do. Earnestly hoping to see improvement in her daughter's behavior, Antonia placed a LifeParticle Card under her bed without her knowing it.

Antonia was in for a shock the next morning. As soon as she got up, her daughter started cleaning her whole room without Antonia asking her to do so. Then something even more amazing happened. Her daughter finished cleaning, came out of her room, and gave Antonia a big hug, saying, "Mom, I love you!"

3. Are thinking about a certain person, praying for that person, and sending LifeParticles to that person similar or different?

Since all three are operations of consciousness, they are identical in that they all involve moving energy. The quantity and quality of the LifeParticles differ, however, according to the level of consciousness and intensity of concentration. When you pray for someone, more LifeParticles will go to him or her than when you just think about them. Visualizing LifeParticles being shared with someone directly could be more effective than praying.

For example, suppose your friend is sick. If you pray, "Please heal my friend," your earnest mind could be converted into energy and shared with your friend. Now try adding visualizing LifeParticles to this. You open your MindScreen and, displaying your sick friend on it, send him or her bright, healthy LifeParticles. You imagine LifeParticles entering and healing where your friend has discomfort, and you see your friend becoming healthier and smiling brightly. You could also do this visualization while you pray. The more concretely you visualize LifeParticles operating, the better their effects are manifested.

4. If I sent LifeParticles to a person, but that person showed no signs of improvement, what is the problem? Have I done something wrong? Or did the LifeParticles not reach him/her?

There could be different factors involved, so let's take a look at each of them.

The first factor is the consciousness of the person who is sending. Did you send LifeParticles with a sincere desire for the other person to get better? Or did you send LifeParticles through thought alone, without having a pure, true heart?

Always check your own intentions and return to purity, unconditional love, and compassion.

The second factor is the consciousness of the person who is receiving. Do they, perhaps, have negativity or repulsion concerning the action of energy? If the other person's negativity is too strong, it could have canceled the effects of the LifeParticles you sent. At such times, try to open the other person's heart through other forms of action, like a friendly word or smile, and establish a connection between the two of you. If a heart-to-heart connection established between you is based on mutual trust, LifeParticles will be conveyed more rapidly and powerfully because they are an effect of consciousness.

The third factor is time. It would be great if the effects appeared after just a few times, but the time required varies with your concentration and the other person's condition. An earnest heart, it is said, can move heaven and earth. It's important to send LifeParticles continuously with a sincere heart.

One thing to keep in mind is that, in any situation, we can only do our best; we have to understand that we cannot control others as we want. It's not good to blame yourself, the other person, or the environment, just because you didn't get the results you wanted. The reason we do LifeParticle Meditation is to cause positive change, and to experience our own essence, which is love.

5. Is it possible for LifeParticles to cure any disease?

Although there are people who have had miraculous experiences through LifeParticle Meditation, these results became realities for them due to a combination of their powerful belief and various other conditions. This can't be applied universally. Naturally, a person who is sick should get treatment from a medical professional. It's all right to use LifeParticle Meditation as a supplementary means of treatment to ensure circulation of bright, healthy energy, but you must remember that LifeParticle Meditation cannot replace professional diagnosis and treatment by a competent professional.

6. I keep feeling resentment for a certain person. Does bad energy go to that person if I have this kind of attitude? Does LifeParticle Meditation also help with escaping from that sort of mind-set?

Your thoughts become energy. If you have resentment in your heart, that energy goes to the other person. Your energy could affect the flow of the other person's energy if his or her energy happens to be weak. The other person may temporarily feel energetic effects like tightness and heaviness in the chest or feelings of malaise. If the other person's consciousness is bright and strong, though, he won't be influenced much, since his energy state would offset your energy.

What is important here is that resenting someone else

actually hurts you. To use an extreme analogy, it's as if you drank poison and hoped for someone else to die. Your consciousness darkens if you harbor resentment for someone else. It causes your energy to stagnate and impedes your body's energy circulation. Your heart chakra closes up, so you feel heaviness and constriction in your chest. Though you meditate, in this condition you will have trouble connecting with the LifeParticle Sun.

When you develop resentment, first check the root of your feelings. Sometimes these emotions may not actually be resentment for the other person; they may arise out of a love that hopes to see him or her do well. If that's the case, then try to choose a way to express those feelings through conversation or in some other form beside resentment. In addition, try to understand the person. If you examine things from the other person's perspective, instead of your own, you will be able to understand why they did what they did. If the other person really was at fault, then try to have compassion. Understand that there must have been some reason for their behavior, something that originated in their inner or outer environment, which kept them from being able to control themselves.

When resentment becomes energy and builds up in your body, try to recover your zero point and purify that energy through LifeParticle Meditation. Remove stagnant energy through Chakra Vibration and activate all of your body's energy. Bring a LifeParticle Card close to your heart, and then liver, as these organs are especially influenced by the energy of anger and resentment. Visualize bright LifeParticles coming out of the card, healing the organs and driving away dark energy. Exhale through your mouth, saying, "Hooo . . .," and continually expel the energy of anger from your heart and liver. When your heart feels more peaceful and a smile comes to your face, send bright LifeParticles to the other person, too.

7. After sharing LifeParticles with another person, wouldn't I lose some of my own LifeParticles?

No; in fact, you could actually receive more LifeParticles because your benevolent intention calls loving LifeParticles to you. When you want to send bright LifeParticles to another person, you visualize receiving the light of the LifeParticle Sun above your head and then sharing it with the other person. The brighter and more numerous the LifeParticles you send, the brighter and more numerous are the LifeParticles you receive. You can't help it. When you send LifeParticles, the energy of pure love for another activates your heart chakra. And by visualizing on your MindScreen, you end up sensitizing your brain more and enhancing your creative power for manifesting what you want.

It is often said that giving is receiving. This wisdom is especially true in the case of LifeParticles. Elevating and focusing your consciousness to send LifeParticles to another person is itself a wonderful, self-rewarding form of LifeParticle Meditation that helps you even more.

Acknowledgments

For her significant assistance in writing this book, I heartily thank Hyerin Moon. I'd also like to extend my sincere appreciation to Daniel Graham for translating it from Korean to English, and to Mary McLean for her thoughtful editing. I also wish to thank all of the people at BEST Life Media who worked hard to make this book a reality. It was a labor of love.

In putting together *LifeParticle Meditation*, many people who use LifeParticles shared their wonderful stories with me. I offer them my gratitude. They are a constant inspiration to me. I hope they can inspire you as well.

About Ilchi Lee

Ilchi Lee is an impassioned visionary, educator, mentor, and innovator; he has dedicated his life not only to teaching energy principles but also to researching and developing methods to nurture the full potential of the human brain.

For over thirty years, his life's mission has been to empower people and to help them harness their own creative power and personal potential. To help individuals achieve that goal, he has developed many successful mind–body training methods, including Dahn Yoga and Brain Education. His principles and methods have inspired many people around the world to live healthier and happier lives.

Lee is a *New York Times* bestselling author who has penned thirty-four books, including *The Call of Sedona: Journey of the Heart*, *Healing Society: A Prescription for Global Enlightenment*, and *Brain Wave Vibration: Getting Back into the Rhythm of a Happy, Healthy Life*.

He is also a well-respected humanitarian who has been working with the United Nations and other organizations for global peace. Lee serves as the president of the University of Brain Education and the International Brain Education Association. For more information about Ilchi Lee and his work, visit www.ilchi.com.

Learn More about LifeParticles

Online Resources

You can find a wealth of information about LifeParticles on www.lifeparticle.com. This website was designed to share the power and possibilities of LifeParticles through meditation while bringing together a community of like-minded people. On this website, you can watch the movie *Change: The LifeParticle Effect*, find information on Energy Meditation Circles, and meet many enthusiastic individuals who are practicing LifeParticle Meditation. Conceived by Ilchi Lee, this online education hub provides enriching live broadcasting and videos on demand of guided meditations and mindful living tips that anyone can use anytime, anywhere.

Instructors and Meditation Centers

If you would like to learn LifeParticle Meditation from an experienced instructor, please find a nearby Dahn Yoga or Body + Brain Holistic Yoga center. LifeParticle principles and meditation are taught at over 1,000 locations worldwide, including 120 centers in the United States. In addition to LifeParticle Meditation, they offer group classes and individual sessions in meditative movement and breathing, as well as personal growth workshops. To find a Dahn Yoga center near you, visit www.dahnyoga.com or call 877-477-YOGA. For Body + Brain Holistic Yoga Centers, go to www.bodynbrain.com or call 480-664-2194.

Helpful Books and CDs

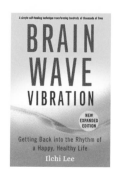

Brain Wave Vibration
Getting Back into the Rhythm of a Happy, Healthy Life
By Ilchi Lee, Paperback, $14.95

Brain Wave Vibration is the most frequently used warm-up exercise for LifeParticle Meditation because of its simplicity and effectiveness. Learn how to move your body to your own natural healing rhythm to slow down and integrate your brain waves. Based on the premise that our brain waves affect every level of our health, this easy method can help you manage stress, rediscover your physical vitality, and stimulate your natural healing ability.

LifeParticle Energy Meditation CD
By Ilchi Lee, Guided Meditation CD, $19.95

Designed by Ilchi Lee and spoken by Jawn McKinley, this guided meditation CD will help you to experience the transformative nature of LifeParticles. The first half of this CD consists of meditation exercises for activating the chakras and the body's entire energy system so you can more fully access LifeParticles. The second half provides meditation techniques for experiencing unity with the source of life and accelerating self-healing.

LifeParticle Sound Healing CD
By Ilchi Lee, Music CD, $19.95

This CD is especially for people who seek vibration music for their LifeParticle Meditation. The sounds of crystal bowls, gongs, flutes, and other instruments, played by Ilchi Lee, will generate subtle yet powerful vibrations throughout your whole body. These vibrations will calm your mind, activate the body's energy centers, and allow LifeParticles to flow powerfully through your body.

How to Use the LifeParticle Card

Please take out the LifeParticle Card to the right after carefully cutting an edge of the plastic vinyl cover with a knife.

Please refer to chapter 9 of this book for general explanation and usage of the LifeParticle Card, and chapters 11, 12, and 13 for its application in different meditation settings.

If you would like to order more LifeParticle Cards, please visit www.lifeparticle.com.